Y0-BBW-046

MOONSHINE

MOONSHINE

A CULTURAL HISTORY OF AMERICA'S INFAMOUS LIQUOR

JAIME JOYCE

ZENITH
PRESS

ACKNOWLEDGMENTS

I'd like to thank Erik Gilg for making this project happen and the
New York Public Library for being the irreplaceable resource that it is.
I'm also grateful for the assistance of several people:
Mari Keiko Gonzalez, Don Heiny, Paco Joyce, Tami Brockway Joyce,
Bartram Nason, Katy Olson, and Ginia Sweeney. Thank you all so
much. Cheers!

First published in 2014 by Zenith Press, an imprint of Quarto Publishing Group USA Inc.,
400 First Avenue North, Suite 400, Minneapolis, MN 55401 USA

Zenith Press titles are also available at discounts in bulk quantity for industrial or sales-promotional use.
For details write to Special Sales Manager at Quarto Publishing Group USA Inc., 400 First Avenue North,
Suite 400, Minneapolis, MN 55401 USA.

To find out more about our books, visit us online at www.zenithpress.com.

ISBN-13: 978-0-7603-4584-9

Library of Congress Cataloging-in-Publication Data
Joyce, Jaime, 1971-
  Moonshine : a cultural history of America's infamous liquor / by Jaime Joyce.
     pages cm
  ISBN 978-0-7603-4584-9 (hardback)
  1. Drinking of alcoholic beverages--United States--History. 2. Distilling, Illicit--United States--History. I. Title.
  GT2893.J69 2014
  663'.5--dc23
                           2013047071

Editor: Erik Gilg
Design Manager: James Kegley
Cover Designer: John Barnett
Layout Designer: Brenda Canales

Printed in China
10 9 8 7 6 5 4 3 2

TABLE OF CONTENTS

PROLOGUE Bangin' in the Woods   6

1   "The Pernicious Practice of Distilling"
    in Early America   16

2   Whiskey Rebels, "Watermelon Armies,"
    and President Washington   28

3   War on Whiskey: Taxing Liquor
    and Defying the Law in the 1800s   42

4   Prohibition's Rise and Fall,
    and What Happened in Between   60

5   Moonshine on Trial   74

6   "Death Defying Ding-Dong Daddies
    from the Realm of Speed":
    Moonshine and the Birth of NASCAR   88

7   "Popskull Crackdown"   106

8   Moonshine Renaissance   122

9   Making Mountain Dew   142

10 Moonshine in Pop Culture   154

EPILOGUE Moonshiners Reunion   168

NOTES & SOURCES   177

PHOTO & MUSIC CREDITS   200

INDEX   204

BANGIN'
IN THE WOODS

Well, the deacon drove by in his auto so shined,
Said his family was down with the flu.
And he thought that I ought to get him a quart
Of that good old mountain dew.

—Bascom Lamar Lunsford, "Good Old Mountain Dew," 1928
(recorded in 1947 by country artist Grandpa Jones
and covered by the alternative rock band Ween
on their 1999 concert album *Paintin' the Town Brown:*
Ween Live '90–'98)

Hanging on a white-pine-paneled wall inside Dawsonville Moonshine Distillery, in Dawsonville, Georgia, is a large, framed photograph of an **Appalachian moonshiner.** The old man is seated beneath a tree in a high-back chair nestled in a thicket of tall grass, looking country sharp in blue denim Red Camel overalls, a plaid shirt buttoned up tight to the collar, and a little brown crumpled hat, the type that people in these parts refer to as a moonshiner's bonnet. His pose—chin up, unsmiling, head turned halfway to a silhouette, while gripping a flask of clear corn whiskey with both hands, one on the body, the other on its neck—suggests a craftsman's pride. It also looks as if he's about to twist off the lid and take a sip.

In a different setting, the portrait might seem like a marketing gimmick. But here, it's personal history. The man in the photograph is a Georgia moonshiner of some renown, by the name of Simmie Free. He was Cheryl Wood's granddad, and Dawsonville Moonshine Distillery is Cheryl Wood's baby. She opened the place in 2012, after nearly a decade in management at AT&T. "It was my family business forever, but it was an illegal family business," Wood says of making moonshine. "I had an idea to take it legal."

Wood also had the idea to open the business in the same building as Dawsonville City Hall, which also happens to be in the same building as the Georgia Racing Hall of Fame, a shrine to local legends like Lloyd Seay and Roy Hall, both of whom got their start running homemade liquor from Dawson County to shot joints in Atlanta, some 60 miles to the south. So Wood—a friendly blonde, whose nickname, "Happy," sums up her cheerful demeanor—met with mayor Joe Lane Cox, and made her pitch. "He thought the town needed it," Wood says. "He called it the missing piece."

The plan made perfect sense. Decades ago, Dawson County earned the title Moonshine Capital of the World for the unusually large number of stills uncovered in the area by federal revenue agents, and since 1967, Dawsonville, the county seat, has hosted each fall the Mountain Moonshine Festival. One highlight of the annual event is a parade of vintage cars—mostly Fords, which were popular for their powerful V-8 engines—the very ones that once sailed through the hills on the way to market, tail ends heavy with the weight of Mason jars and gallon-size tin cans filled with liquid corn. Always notably absent from the festival, however, has been legal moonshine.

Legal moonshine, of course, is something of an oxymoron. By definition, moonshine is liquor for which taxes have not been paid. Purists say it's made from corn, though moonshine can and has been produced using nearly anything that ferments. *Moonshine* is used to describe a beverage made at night—by the light of the moon—in an attempt to avoid detection by law enforcement agents eager to arrest shiners and bust up their stills. Another definer: Moonshine is unaged— young and raw. It's clear, like vodka or gin, not amber or brown, like whiskey, which is matured in white-oak barrels to mellow the taste and give the spirit color. Moonshine has been described as whiskey without the wood. Traditionally, it's associated with the South.

Today, moonshine has entered the mainstream. A growing number of legal distilleries, big and small, across the United States, from Brooklyn, New York, to Seattle, Washington, to Buena Vista, Colorado, are making it. Drinkers are eager for a taste of America's homegrown spirit, and if it's made by small producers out of locally sourced ingredients, the appeal is even greater.

Some distillers, like Heather Shade of the upstart Port Chilkoot Distillery in Haines, Alaska, call their product moonshine and embrace the drink's renegade past. "It's a new product that's giving a tribute to a traditional one," Shade says, rejecting the literalism of critics who contend that if you're paying taxes on your whiskey you can't call it moonshine.

Other distillers market their unaged whiskey as *white dog* or *white lightning*—both synonyms for *moonshine*. Heaven Hill Distilleries, in Bardstown, Kentucky, which distributes a diverse range of spirits, including Evan Williams bourbon and Hpnotiq, a candy-colored French liqueur, goes for the more precise terminology, calling its line of white dogs "new make," as in whiskey fresh from the still, untouched by the barrel.

Corn whiskey at Dawsonville Moonshine Distillery is made from a 150-year-old family recipe passed down through Simmie Free by fourth-generation moonshiner Dwight Bearden, who's known as "Punch." Bearden says he picked up the nickname as a young man after getting into a fistfight with federal agents who wanted to send him to the penitentiary for making illegal liquor. When asked how he learned his trade, he likes to tell people he read about it in a book. Press him a bit, though, and Bearden admits that he's been "tinkering around stills" since he was about 6 or 7 years old.

"The moonshine helped feed me when I was a young boy," Bearden says. When he was growing up, there were few jobs in this corner of the Appalachians, and people did what they could to support themselves and their families. To see him at the distillery, with his thick silver beard and overalls, using a long wooden stick to stir up a bubbling hot vat of mash—a mixture of water, ground corn, and malt—it's not hard to imagine Bearden making shine right alongside Simmie Free, somewhere off in the nearby hills, under a protective tree canopy of hickory, oak, and pine.

As much as the moonshine business has changed since Free's time, the basics remain the same. Dawsonville Moonshine Distillery owner Cheryl Wood says her grain is a "very, very, old-timey corn, not genetically modified." She gets it from a local farmer whose family has supplied north Georgia moonshiners for three generations, and malts it herself—moistening the yellow, white, and burgundy-colored kernels to get them to germinate, or sprout, then drying them, thus prepping the grain to convert its starch into sugar while brewing. At the end of the distilling process, spent mash is carted off and used as feed for hogs and cattle on nearby farms.

Wood takes pride in her recipe. One ingredient she won't use is sugar. During Prohibition, moonshiners began to add sugar to the mash to quicken the fermentation process and stretch the yield, and before long, moonshine went from being corn whiskey to nothing but sugar liquor. "If it has too much sugar it's really gonna burn up front" when you drink it, Wood says. Moonshine made by Dawsonville Distillery is different, she adds. "When you swish it in your mouth, you can actually taste the corn, and not just the alcohol," Wood says. Bearden agrees. Take a sip and you get "a warm glow all the way down your throat and into your stomach."

In 2013, the Beverage Tasting Institute (BTI), in Chicago, awarded Dawsonville Distillery's Georgia Corn Whiskey a silver medal in its International Review of Spirits competition. "That's a biggie," Wood says. "We were all jumping up and down." On its website, BTI gives Dawsonville moonshine an 89 rating ("Highly Recommended") and describes it as having "grainy aromas of roasted cornhusk and bread with hints of dried apple, nut, and clay with a silky, dry-yet-fruity medium body and a nuanced finish with notes of flowers and pears."

That's fancy language for a beverage born in the backwoods, a drink with a long history of evocative epithets including *rot gut*, *panther piss*, and *fire water*, and often recalled with displeasure by people who long ago and one-time-only took a taste from a jar passed around at a frat party. Times have changed. Today, some people prefer to sip moonshine neat, nothing added, while newcomers are often initiated by way of mixed drinks. To make a "Moon-a-rita," Wood uses Dawsonville moonshine in place of tequila. At the 2013 Atlanta Film Festival, she served a cocktail made with moonshine, peach schnapps, and cranberry juice. "It's similar to Sex on the Beach [the vodka drink]," Wood says. "But we called it Bangin' in the Woods."

MOON-A-RITA

Ingredients
- 1 6-oz. can frozen limeade
- 1 oz. triple sec
- Splash of lime
- 4 oz. Dawsonville Moonshine Georgia Corn Whiskey

Directions
Fill blender with ice. Add ingredients. Blend until smooth.

BANGIN' IN THE WOODS

Ingredients
- 2 oz. orange juice
- 2 oz. cranberry juice
- 1 oz. peach schnapps
- 1½ oz. Dawsonville Moonshine Georgia Corn Whiskey

Directions
Mix and serve.

Recipes courtesy of Cheryl Wood, Dawsonville Moonshine Distillery

According to food-science writer Harold McGee in his book *On Food and Cooking: The Science and Lore of the Kitchen*, the art of distilling is believed to have been developed 5,000 years ago by the Mesopotamians as they distilled essential oils by heating a mixture of plants and water in a pot, then collected the condensation that formed on its lid. McGee further notes that in the 4th century BCE, Aristotle wrote of converting seawater into freshwater by applying heat then recapturing the condensed vapor, which had shed its salt in the process.

This principle was later applied to alcohol, which has a lower boiling point than water. Simply put, when a mixture of alcohol and water is heated, the droplets of liquid that form from the vapor are

"An early method of distilling fresh water from salt water at sea," *Pennsylvania Magazine*, 1776.

heavy with alcohol. These droplets are then collected, and what you end up with is a more concentrated product than the original. It was the Chinese who seem to have discovered this neat trick, probably about 2,000 years ago, when alchemists distilled small amounts of alcohol from fermented grain. The process eventually became widespread, and by the 13th century, alcohol made from grain was commonly produced and enjoyed by the Chinese people.

In Salerno, Italy, around 1100, distilled alcohol was made for medicinal purposes. By 1300, writes McGee, the scholar Arnaud de Villanova applied the term *aqua vitae*, or "water of life," to distilled wine. Scottish and Irish monks used the same term, in Gaelic, to describe the beverage they were distilling from barley beer. They called it *uisge beatha*, or *usquebaugh (us*-kwih-boh*)*. The term then morphed into the English word *whiskey*. Today, in Scotland and Canada, *whiskey* is spelled without an *e*, while in Ireland and the U.S., it's generally spelled with an *e*.

Records show that whiskey was made in Scotland as early as 1494. The evidence is in the Exchequer roll of that year, in which a request is made for "VIII bolls of malt" from which "to make

A group of men gather around a still in the woods, *Harper's Weekly*, December 7, 1867.

aquavitae." Drying the malted barley over a peat fire lent Scottish whiskeys a distinctive smoky flavor.

In Ireland in 1622, the government imposed a tax on whiskey. Farmers called the beverage "poteen" for the "little pot," or pot still, in which it was made. Not surprisingly, the tax didn't go over well. To many people, it made little sense to pay money to the government for a beverage produced for personal use only, made from grain sown and nurtured on one's own land. Makers with no intention of paying the tax became some of the world's first moonshiners.

In Colonial America, a whiskey-making tradition came ready-made with the arrival of Scots-Irish settlers from Northern Ireland's Ulster region, beginning in the 1700s. They brought with them their taste for the drink and an understanding of how to make it. They may also have brought their copper stills on board the ships that carried

WHAT'S IN A NAME?

Moonshine goes by many names, including *mountain dew*, *catdaddy*, and *hooch*. The latter comes from the word *hoochinoo*, which was the name for liquor distilled from a mash of molasses or sugar, along with flour, potatoes, and yeast, by the Hoochinoo Indians, a Tlingit tribe from Alaska. It's believed that the Hoochinoo were taught to make the liquor in the late 1800s by a whaling-ship deserter. Old oilcans were used as stills. For the worm, or the part of the distilling apparatus through which steam passes during the liquor-making process, the Alaskan natives used either a musket barrel or the long hollowed-out stem of bull kelp, a common seaweed.

them across the Atlantic. Many of these early immigrants put down roots first in Pennsylvania, spreading out in the late 1700s and early 1800s to Virginia, West Virginia, the Carolinas, Kentucky, Tennessee, and Georgia. Like their forebears, they made whiskey, which they enjoyed fresh from the still. The practice of aging whiskey in oak barrels would come later. Exactly when and why is unknown, though a commonly told origin story in the U.S. points to the 1790s, with distillers shipping white whiskey in barrels on flatboats down the Mississippi and Ohio rivers, from Kentucky to New Orleans, where recipients enjoyed the taste of the softer, more mature beverage produced in transit.

Cheryl Wood, of Dawsonville Moonshine Distillery, traces her roots to Scots-Irish immigrants. In the old days, she says, her people used whiskey as medicine, just like the original distillers in Europe. It was useful as both an antiseptic and a painkiller. Camphor oil was added to moonshine to make a rub for aches and pains. When Wood was a child, moonshine doubled as a cough suppressant and sore-throat treatment. To get little ones to tolerate whiskey, adults added something special to the cup: "It was pretty common with everybody in the mountains to put the old-fashioned peppermint-stick candy in it," says Wood. Dwight Bearden, her distiller, says that in the early 1980s, when his daughter was small and sick with a cold, the family doctor prescribed a tablespoonful of apple brandy or corn whiskey, whatever the Beardens had on hand. "My wife looked fit to be tied," when she heard that, Bearden says. But the remedy worked.

Simmie Free (Cheryl Wood's moonshiner grandfather) claimed to drink corn whiskey nearly every day of his life, telling author Joseph Earl Dabney, in an interview for the book *More Mountain Spirits*, that moonshine was the only thing that kept him alive. He started making it while still a child. "I went to helpin' my daddy make likker when I wuddn't but nine years old," he told Dabney. "My daddy just let me go to the still with him and I watched him and learnt it myself."

Over the years, the law mostly left Free alone. But he wasn't always lucky. On at least four occasions, he served time in jail and in prison for violating liquor laws and evading taxes. But as it turned out, being locked up wasn't bad for business. "That's a good place to get customers," Wood says of her granddad's time behind bars. "He would just take orders and fill them when he got out."

Simmie Free died in 1980 at the age of 88. How would he feel about his granddaughter taking the family business legit? He probably wouldn't be too thrilled about her having to hand over tax money to the government. After all, moonshiners have generally been of the opinion that taxes have already been paid on the materials used to make their whiskey, and that it didn't make sense to collect it twice. But, Wood says, he would have loved to see her distillery in action: "To be able to do [this] and not hide, oh, let me tell you, he would be super, super excited."

"THE PERNICIOUS PRACTICE OF DISTILLING" IN EARLY AMERICA

"No man ever became suddenly a drunkard."

—Benjamin Rush, MD, *An Inquiry into the Effects of Ardent Spirits upon the Human Body and Mind*, 1823 edition

To understand the rise of moonshine whiskey and its place in American history, it helps to understand the country's relationship with liquor and to know something about how the nation's drinking habits and attitudes toward booze have changed over time. A fun starting point is an experiment conducted by writer Sarah Lohman, of Brooklyn, New York. Here's what she did.

As a way to usher in 2012, Lohman bucked the health resolutions that so often mark the New Year and instead gave herself a bibulous challenge. For one day, Lohman drank like a Colonial American, which is to say that she drank a lot and at hours that might seem strange even to an alcoholic or a college student. She wrote about the experience on her blog, *Four Pounds Flour*, which focuses on 18th- and 19th-

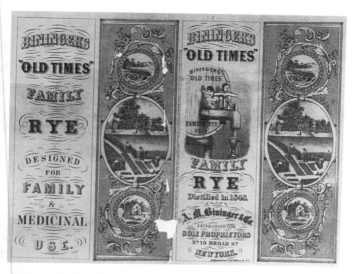

Founded in New York City in the 1700s, the Bininger distillery touted its rye whiskey as a family health tonic.

century American food and drink. Lohman's January 5 blog post is titled, well, "Drink Like a Colonial American Day."

At 8:30 a.m., Lohman began with a beverage of sugar, whiskey, water, and bitters. (In Colonial times, bitters, a blend of herbs and spices infused in high-proof alcohol, were thought to have health-giving properties. Today, bitters are a key ingredient in cocktails.) After that, she and her boyfriend accompanied bacon, eggs, and toast with a tall mug of hard cider. Made from fermented apples, cider was a crowd pleaser in the 1700s. Diluted, it was given to children. "Yes, I'm a little drunk," Lohman posted at 9:38 a.m. (Of note, the cider Lohman drank was only 5% alcohol by volume; in Colonial times, the alcohol content of cider would have been twice that.)

At 11:00 a.m.: "It is now the 'elevens'!!! The Colonial American equivalent of a coffee break!" Lohman wrote. She fixed herself a hot toddy with apple brandy. At 1:19 p.m.: "I'm hungover and it's painful." For lunch around 2:00, Lohman heated up a DiGiorno frozen pizza and consumed it with 12 ounces of hard cider. During the meal, she considered the schedule she'd need to keep up for the rest of the day to complete her booze-soaked exercise. With an early dinner, there would be more cider, followed by another small meal with drinks and a spirited nightcap. It was a dizzying agenda. After lunch, Lohman kicked back on the couch, turned on her TV, and quickly fell asleep. She woke up with a migraine. Her post at 5:48 p.m.: "That's it. I'm calling it. I can't continue."

The result of Lohman's experiment, aside from a killer hangover, was an up-close-and-personal view of our hard-drinking ancestors. What would be considered heavy consumption today used to be common. It's estimated that in 1770, Colonial Americans 15 years and older each drank 7 gallons of spirits, 0.2 gallons of wine, and 34 gallons of hard cider a year. That translates into 6.6 gallons of pure alcohol. Compare that to recent government figures, which show that in 2011, per capita consumption of pure alcohol for individuals 14 and older stood at 2.28 gallons.

In 1620, the Pilgrims carried alcohol with them on their voyage to the New World. Provisions on the *Mayflower* included salted meats, cured fish, butter, cheese, and barrels of beer. Alcohol was believed to give men energy, which they'd need for working the colony's rough and untamed land. Not only that—beer was considered safer and more wholesome than the water in Plymouth, which often was muddied or polluted or tasted of iron.

Drinking was part of everyday life. Drunkenness, however, was frowned upon. Colonial leaders saw it as a threat to their settlements. Some passed laws against it. Others called for an outright ban on alcohol. Drunkards faced fines and punishments, including public whipping. Some were sentenced to confinement in stocks.

John Winthrop, while on board the *Arbella* as it sailed from England to New England, in the spring of 1630, wrote in his journal about the problem of alcohol. "A maid servant in the ship, being stomach sick, drank so much strong water, that she was senseless, and had near killed herself," he noted in an entry dated May 3. He continued, musing on his discussions with shipmates: "We observed it a common fault in our young people, that they gave themselves to drink hot waters very immoderately." Three years later, as governor of the Massachusetts Bay Colony, Winthrop wrote about a settler who faced one of the most humiliating consequences of indulgence: "Robert Cole, having been oft punished for drunkenness, was now ordered to wear a red D about his neck for a year."

But punishing drunks didn't keep them from drinking. In 1654, the Massachusetts Bay Colony tried to curtail alcohol use with a law aimed at tavern owners, innkeepers, and ordinary citizens:

> None licensed to sell strong waters, nor any private housekeeper, shall permit any person or persons to sit tippling strong waters, wine, or strong beer in their houses, under severe penalties—for the first offence twenty shillings, and in default of payment to be set in the stocks; for the second

offence, twenty shillings and forfeiture of license; for the third, to be put under a twenty pound bond for good behavior, with two sufficient sureties, or be committed to prison.

Where did the colonists get all this alcohol? Beer was imported from England, while wine, enjoyed by wealthier settlers, sailed on ships from Spain and France. It wasn't long, however, before colonists, not content to await shipments from the motherland, took the do-it-yourself approach. By the 1630s, they'd already begun to brew their own beer, and to ferment and distill native fruits and other ingredients. "We can make liquor to sweeten our lips, / Of pumpkins, and parsnips, and walnut-tree chips," went a catchy rhyme. Hard cider was a particular favorite. It was part of the social fabric, the quaff of weddings, funerals, meetings, and other events of daily life.

George Thorpe is the first colonist known to have distilled a beverage from corn, though his operation was short-lived, and most likely for personal use only. In 1620, Thorpe, an English minister, set up his still at Jamestown, Virginia, and wrote about his endeavors in a letter to his English cousin: "Wee have found a waie to make soe good drink of Indian corne I have divers times refused to drinke good stronge English beare and chose to drinke that." Two years later, Powhatan Indians killed Thorpe and more than 300 settlers in a raid. Noted among Thorpe's belongings was "a copper still, old."

In 1640, William Kieft, director-general of the Dutch colony of New Netherland, established Colonial America's first distillery. Located in Staten Island, New York, the distillery produced brandy, which is made from fruit. Probably apples, in Kieft's case. Some accounts, however, say it wasn't brandy Kieft was cooking up, but whiskey, which is a spirit distilled from grain. Most likely, that grain was leftover slop from brewing beer. By 1664, the Dutch colony had been taken over by the British, who renamed the settlement New York, and because grain was scarce and people were hungry, an act was passed in 1676 sharply limiting the distillation of grain for liquor. Whiskey would have to wait.

The stage had been set for the ascendance of rum. Colonial distilling revolved around it, and by the mid 1600s there existed a swift trade between Massachusetts, Rhode Island, New York, and Pennsylvania, and the Caribbean, where sugarcane was grown and harvested and turned into molasses, the thick, sweet syrup used to make the drink. New World settlers developed a taste for rum. At first, the drink was imported from the West Indies. But soon enough, distilleries cropped up in the Colonies. In Boston, plants were established on Essex, South, and Beach streets. One of the city's earliest distilleries, run by Henry Hill, was founded in 1714. In New York City, by 1746, there were three distilleries, and three more were in operation by 1749. At one point in the 1700s, Newport, Rhode Island, claimed 30 distilleries. All of them were pumping out rum. In Massachusetts alone, a 1717 report said the colony was producing 200,000 gallons of rum a year. And in 1734, it was estimated that annual consumption of rum by individual colonists was 3.75 U.S. gallons.

There was, however, a dark side to rum, and it went far beyond intemperance, for rum played a key role in the so-called triangular trade: Distilleries in Boston and Newport had sugar and molasses shipped in from the Caribbean, and the rum they produced was then shipped to Africa, where it was exchanged for slaves. Enslaved Africans would then be sent to the islands to work the sugarcane fields. Author Daniel Dorchester, in his 1884 book *The Liquor Problem in All Ages*, described the relationship between rum and the slave trade, calling it "a fitting conjunction of two monstrous evils in the most diabolical of all outrages against humanity."

Still, the appetite colonists had for rum was boundless, and it showed in the lengths they were willing to go to keep the liquor flowing. When Britain imposed the Molasses Act, in 1733, in an attempt to discourage imports of molasses from the French and Dutch West Indies, colonists began a contraband trade with the French. They

FLIP: A COLONIAL FAVORITE

This recipe for rum flip appeared in Jerry Thomas's 1862 cocktail bible, *How to Mix Drinks, or The Bon-Vivant's Companion.* It's likely that the resulting beverage is similar in composition and taste to a flip that would have been served in taverns during America's Colonial period. Here is Thomas's description:

> Keep grated ginger and nutmeg with a little fine dried lemon peel, rubbed together in a mortar. To make a quart of flip:— Put the ale on the fire to warm, and beat up three or four eggs with four ounces of moist sugar, a teaspoonful of grated nutmeg or ginger, and a gill [four ounces] of good old rum or brandy. When the ale is near to boil, put it into one pitcher, and the rum and eggs, &c., into another; turn it from one pitcher to another till it is as smooth as cream.

again resorted to illegal trading, in 1760, with the imposition of the Sugar Act, which placed a tax on molasses of six cents per gallon.

The demand for rum was simply too great for colonists to allow the British to put a pinch on their supply. Everyone from pastors to farmers to children took a liking to the drink, and it was used both as an elixir and an intoxicant. Doctors prescribed rum steeped with tansy flower to soothe a cough. Mixed with the mossy-looking liverwort plant, it was a remedy for gallstones. Tavern keepers used the liquor to whip up drinks like punch and "flip," which was made from a blend of rum, brandy, sugar, and eggs, then heated with the tip of a hot poker, or flip iron.

Observing the excessive use of alcohol for non-medicinal purposes, Benjamin Franklin, a noted Renaissance man who would go on to become one of the country's Founding Fathers, compiled *The Drinker's Dictionary.* Published in the *Pennsylvania Gazette* on January 13, 1737, when Franklin was just 31 years old, his compendium included nearly 300 colorful words and phrases that could be used to call a man drunk. Some, like *addled*, *afflicted*, *boozy*, *glaiz'd*, *hammerish*, and *tipsey*, are familiar to modern ears. A few are real gems, ripe for revival: *jambled*, *juicy*, *staggerish*, *stew'd*, and *double-tonge'd*. Among the other entries: *Got corns in his head*; *Rais'd his monuments*; and *Sir Richard has taken off his considering cap*.

During the French and Indian War (1756–1763), the Colonies supplied Britain with troops, and the British, in turn, supplied the troops with rations of rum. So sought-after was liquor that rum sellers made a living by shadowing troops as they moved from one encampment to the next. At least one military leader, however, came to view alcohol as having an ill effect on his men, and he promised to punish by lashing those who purchased it from traveling salesmen.

By war's end, demand for rum was even more robust, and the colonists' drinking problem did not escape the notice of America's first Continental Congress. In 1774, this political body made clear its opinion on the matter:

> Resolved, That it be recommended to the several Legislatures of the United Colonies immediately to pass laws the more effectually to put a stop to the pernicious practice of distilling, by which the most extensive evils are likely to be derived, if not quickly prevented.

Yet with the onset of the Revolutionary War, the Continental Congress voted that distilled spirits should be supplied to the troops as a daily ration. So it was that on December 13, 1777, just days after a tough engagement with British troops, General George Washington issued orders meant to comfort the battle-weary forces as they settled into a Pennsylvania campsite near the Schuylkill River. "A gill of whiskey is to be issued immediately to each officer, soldier, and waggoner," he wrote.

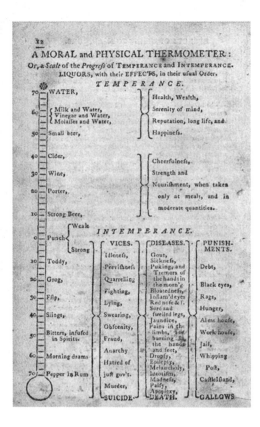

During the war, the Colonies were cut off from imports of foreign-made beer, wine, and spirits—and the molasses needed to make rum. In response, colonial distillers turned to whiskey made from homegrown barley, rye, and corn to satisfy the demand for drink. The consumption of grain for booze was so great that people began to worry that the army would soon face famine, and in 1779, Pennsylvania passed a law banning the use of grain for distillation, hearkening back to restrictions imposed in New York some 100 years earlier.

Restrictions on whiskey making didn't last long, however. After America gained its independence from Britain, the newly formed country was awash in alcohol. Prominent people expressed concern about it. In 1784, Benjamin Rush, a Philadelphia physician, professor at the University of Pennsylvania, and signer of the Declaration of Independence, published *An Enquiry into the Effects of Spirituous Liquors Upon the Human Body*. The work was reprinted several times, with slight changes to the title, and later editions included an illustrated "moral and physical thermometer" designed to show the progress from temperance to intemperance. In an 1823 version the thermometer shows that water, milk, and "small beer" were associated with good health, serenity, and long life. Cider, wine, and "strong beer," enjoyed in small amounts and with meals, Rush equated with "cheerfulness, strength and nourishment."

Rush's thermometer, however, linked the use of strong alcoholic liquors such as gin, rum, and brandy with everything from idleness and sickness to murder, madness, and despair, the latter the result of drinking a dram, or an eighth of an ounce, of spirits in the morning and at night.

Rush went on to describe 12 stages of drunkenness and the symptoms associated with each one of them. In his view, the final stage was most grim, and he began the entry with "certain extravagant acts which indicate a temporary fit of madness":

These are singing, hallooing, roaring, imitating the noises of brute animals, jumping, tearing off clothes, dancing naked, breaking glasses and china, and dashing other articles of household furniture upon the ground, or floor.

From that point on, Rush explained, the inebriate devolved even further:

The face now becomes flushed, the eyes project, and are somewhat watery, winking is less frequent than is natural;

the upper lip is protruded—the head inclines a little to one shoulder—the jaw falls—belching and hiccups take place—the limbs totter—the whole body staggers. . . . He now closes his eyes, and falls into a profound sleep, frequently attended with snoring, and profuse sweats, arid sometimes with such a relaxation of the muscles which confine the bladder and the lower bowels, as to produce a symptom which delicacy forbids me to mention. In this condition he often lies from ten, twelve, and twenty-four hours, to two, three, four, and five days, an object of pity and disgust to his family and friends.

Drunkenness wasn't pretty, and Rush's ideas were influential. In 1790, Secretary of the Treasury Alexander Hamilton lamented America's liquor problem in Congress, calling for a tax on distilled spirits as a way to both curb drinking and pay down the nation's Revolutionary War debt, which the newly created federal government had assumed from the states:

The consumption of ardent spirits . . . no doubt very much on account of their cheapness, is carried to an extreme, which is truly to be regretted, as well in regard to the health and the morals, as to the economy of the community.

Should the increase of duties tend to a decrease of the consumption of those articles, the effect would be, in every respect, desirable. The saving, which it would occasion, would leave individuals more at their ease, and promote a more favourable balance of trade. As far as this decrease might be applicable to distilled spirits, it would encourage the substitution of cyder and malt liquors, benefit agriculture, and open a new and productive source of revenue.

Hamilton made a persuasive argument. It didn't take long for his plan to become a reality, and on March 3, 1791, the Excise Act went into effect, imposing for the first time in the United States a tax on domestically distilled spirits. In 1791, spirits were practically synonymous with whiskey. Many of the distillers making the drink were farmers from western Pennsylvania. Of Scots-Irish descent, they carried with them a strong distilling tradition. A lot of people were against the whiskey tax, including Pennsylvania senator William Maclay. "It is the most execrable system that ever was framed against the liberty of a people," he wrote. "War and bloodshed are the most likely consequence of all this." His words foretold a dark period in American history.

LAY OFF THE WINE, MR. HAMILTON

Alexander Hamilton was not an abstainer. Born on the island of Nevis, in the British West Indies, on January 11, 1755 (or 1757—no one knows for sure), he emigrated to New York in 1773 as a teenager and went on to become secretary of the Treasury under President George Washington, in 1789. Although he advocated for and secured a tax on distilled spirits, in part because of what he saw as their deleterious effects on health, Hamilton didn't shy away from alcohol himself. When suffering from a digestive ailment, he was ordered by his doctor to drink no more than three glasses of wine a day. The prescription speaks not only to Hamilton's personal consumption patterns, but it provides perspective on what it meant during Colonial times to drink in moderation.

WHISKEY REBELS, "WATERMELON ARMIES," AND PRESIDENT WASHINGTON

My daddy, he made whiskey
And my granddaddy did too.
We ain't paid no whiskey tax
Since seventeen ninety two.

—Albert Frank Beddoe,
"Copper Kettle," 1953

Early in the morning, on Wednesday, July 16, 1794, a riled-up gang of about 35 men, many of whom were carrying guns, sticks, and clubs, showed up at Bower Hill, the western Pennsylvania mansion of regional tax inspector General John Neville. The men had resolved the previous evening to call on Neville at his home. He'd been spotted making the rounds with a federal marshal who was delivering court summonses to farmers who had failed to register their stills with the United States government. Such registration, and payment for whiskey produced, was required by the distilled-spirits tax that had been passed by Congress three years earlier.

These frontier farmers found the law particularly onerous. For them, distilling grain into whiskey was a practical way to preserve the crop. A pair of eight-gallon kegs on a single packhorse was much easier to move across the rugged Allegheny Mountains to markets in the east than heavy sacks of grain carried by an entire team of animals. On the other side of the range, farmers bartered their whiskey for iron and salt. No cash was exchanged, yet cash was demanded by the government for payment of taxes.

Even more galling were stipulations that seemed to favor distillers east of the Alleghenies, who tended to operate on a larger scale, with stills that were able to produce far more whiskey than those that were run by farmers. By law, distillers who operated in cities, towns, and villages were charged per gallon actually produced, but distillers in rural areas were charged a flat sum based on the number of gallons their stills were capable of producing in a year. Those regulations worked against small-scale farmer-distillers, most of whom didn't operate on the same schedule as their larger counterparts, producing far fewer gallons per year than the government expected them to. For that reason, the government's flat-fee calculation had small distillers paying for more gallons per year than they were putting out. The result: Large-scale distillers paid about nine cents per gallon, while the little guys ended up paying more.

On top of that, many western Pennsylvanians viewed the whiskey tax as just plain offensive. What about personal liberty, they wondered. What business did government inspectors have visiting a farmer's property to examine his still, measure the proof of his product, and stamp a seal upon his wooden kegs? Furthermore, the imposition of the tax reminded many people of a similar tax raised on spirits in Great Britain, the very country from which the new nation had just gained its independence after a long and bloody fight.

Incensed, people in the western counties organized against the excise law and drafted petitions urging its repeal. At a meeting in Pittsburgh, in 1792, attendees issued a document spelling out their feelings—and explaining the punishment they intended to inflict on individuals who signed on as government tax collectors:

A mob tars and feathers a tax collector during the Whiskey Rebellion of 1794.

[We] will consider such persons as unworthy of our friendship, have no intercourse or dealings with them, withdraw from them every assistance, withhold all the comforts of life which depend upon those duties that as man and fellow citizens we owe to each other, and upon all occasions treat them with the contempt they deserve.

That same year, the federal government did make one revision to the law, reducing the tax rate on distilled spirits and offering a monthly, rather than a yearly, license for those who worked their stills part-time. That concession, however, did little to soothe discontent. Many people simply refused to pay the whiskey tax, and they followed through on their pledge to make life difficult for collectors. In fact, they made it downright dangerous. In one instance, a group of 12 armed men in disguise broke into a collector's home, tied him up, and threatened him with hanging before taking him to the woods, where they cut off his hair, stripped him naked, tarred and feathered him, then bound him to a tree, where he was left overnight. Other collectors were similarly terrorized and made to publicly resign their posts or run the risk of further attacks.

John Neville knew he was in trouble when the men surrounded and fired upon him and the marshal. After all, the pair had just served papers on a local farmer, ordering him to pay a fine of $250 and to appear in United States District Court in Philadelphia, some 300 miles away over rough terrain. The farmer later reported that the sight of Neville made his blood boil. It was easy to understand why. For years, Neville, who had been named a general for his service in the Revolutionary War, had been a vocal, high-profile opponent of the Pennsylvania state tax on distilled spirits, levied in 1772. Furthermore, one witness reportedly heard Neville say that an excise man who'd been harassed and assaulted by protestors and forced to leave the county deserved rougher treatment than he got. So it came as both a shock and an insult to some when Neville, in 1791, accepted the appointment by President George Washington to the role of regional tax inspector for Pennsylvania's fourth survey district, which included southwestern Allegheny, Fayette, Washington, and Westmoreland counties, as well as south central Bedford County. Neville, once respected for his service to the country and community, was now seen by many as a traitor.

Faced with an angry mob outside his well-appointed home, with its fine furnishings and carpeted floors, Neville was determined not to be their latest victim. The 63-year-old general had the night before covered his windows with planks of wood as a defensive measure. Now he positioned himself near the glass and fired the first shots. Soon after, blasts rang out from an adjoining building, where Neville's slaves had been stationed and given guns with instructions to shoot. The crossfire continued for about 25 minutes, during which time Neville's wife, his little granddaughter, and a young woman escaped the home unharmed. The insurgents, however, didn't make out as well. Five were wounded; one was killed.

The confrontation didn't end there. The next morning, 500 men marched upon Neville's expansive property, which stood on a mountaintop overlooking log cabins below. Badly outnumbered, Neville's slaves fled the scene. Neville had already gone, leaving his estate to be guarded by a friend and a detachment of 11 military men who'd come the night before from Fort Pitt, in nearby Pittsburgh, to assist. Three protestors approached the house, and a series of signals was exchanged between them and the soldiers. The men first demanded that Neville give up his official papers and commissions, but they were told that the general was not home. After that, they requested that a group of six men be allowed to enter the home and search Neville's belongings. Once again they were refused. The insurgents grew impatient, and soon they opened fire.

Bullets flew for about 15 minutes. A call then came from the house and the firing stopped, prompting the rebel leader to step out from behind the tree from which he'd been shielding himself. At that moment a musket shot came from the mansion, striking the rebel dead with a single ball of lead to the groin.

This wasn't a battlefield casualty. The insurgents saw it as cold-blooded murder, and for them, there would now be no holding back. They resumed firing upon the house and the stables, killing three horses. One man set fire to Neville's barn. Hay and grain and stable gear were tinder for the flames, and the entire estate was soon engulfed. The men who'd come to guard Neville's home surrendered, and Bower Hill was destroyed. Seizing an opportunity, and perhaps eager to celebrate the occasion, a few of the protestors broke into Neville's cellar, stole his whiskey, and proceeded to get drunk.

Whiskey rebels rallied in Braddock's Field on August 1, 1794.

The next day, Neville wrote a letter to Pennsylvania congressman Tench Coxe, in which he related the horror of the attack and made it clear that the status quo was no longer effective. The resistance had reached a new high.

"The blow is struck, which determines that the revenue law cannot be carried into execution, until Government changes their system, and adds considerable force to the measures already adopted; from an easy and convenient situation in life, I am in a few hours reduced to difficulties and distress," Neville wrote.

He continued, "What was yesterday an elegant and highly cultivated farm with every convenience is now a melancholy waste. . . . I am retired into Pittsburgh with my family without a single particle of clothing, furniture of any kind, or personal property, save what we have on our backs."

President Washington was outraged upon hearing news of the attack. Two years had passed since he'd issued a proclamation condemning acts of violence against those whose job it was to collect the tax, and the opposition had only escalated. Now he delivered a serious threat, announcing, on August 7, 1794, that the government was prepared to forcefully put down the Pennsylvania uprising:

> It is in my judgment necessary under the circumstances of the case to take measures for calling forth the militia . . . and to cause the laws to be duly executed; and I have accordingly determined so to do, feeling the deepest regret for the occasion, but withal the most solemn conviction that the essential interests of the Union demand it, that the very existence of Government and the fundamental principles of social order are materially involved in the issue, and that the patriotism and firmness of all good citizens are seriously called upon, as occasions may require, to aid in the effectual suppression of so fatal a spirit. I do hereby command all persons being insurgents as aforesaid, and all others whom it may concern, on or before the 1st day of September next to disperse and retire peaceably to their respective abodes.

Washington, however, was shrewd enough to know that the insurgents would not quietly acquiesce. Their actions thus far had shown a complete disregard for the law and, beyond that, for human decency. Throughout the western counties, there remained many who would accept no compromise, and for whom the singular goal was total abolition of the whiskey tax. Others, however, were more moderate in their approach, and while they decried violence, they were staunchly opposed to the excise. On August 14, just one month after the attack on General Neville's home, they came together in a meeting at Parkinson's Ferry, on a tree-studded bluff overlooking the Monongahela River.

The outdoor gathering attracted about 200 delegates—and even more spectators, some of whom were armed—from the four western counties, plus Bedford County, and Ohio County, Virginia (now West Virginia). The atmosphere was charged. Some of those in attendance made clear their contempt for neighbors who expressed a desire for peaceful compliance with the law. Within view of the open-air meeting, they erected a liberty pole from which flew a bold message: LIBERTY AND NO EXCISE, AND NO ASYLUM FOR COWARDS OR TRAITORS.

But the delegates leading the meeting were eager to put the upheaval of the last three years behind them, to return a sense of calm to their communities. They pressed on in spite of the opposition. It was agreed at the meeting to select a committee of 60 people, one from each of the area townships, to convene again three weeks later, on September 2, at Redstone Old Fort. Most urgent, however, was the selection of 12 representatives to meet with three presidential commissioners sent to the region by Washington to broker an accord.

The 12 representatives and the president's men met in Pittsburgh on August 20. The commissioners offered amnesty for past assaults and other lawless acts, and a reduction on the amount of taxes owed by farmer-distillers. Additionally, they gave the protestors the opportunity to recommend people to be excise collectors, a nod to the General Neville debacle.

Certain terms and conditions applied. In exchange for amnesty, people in the western counties were expected to fully comply with the laws of the United States and to submit to the whiskey tax without protest. They were also expected to renounce violence and threatening behavior.

The representatives were inclined to accept the offer. At the upcoming meeting at Redstone Old Fort, they were to present to their constituents the terms of the deal. The challenge would be getting them to agree, and the odds didn't look good. While negotiations were taking place, rebels pasted an anonymous incitement on a local building and published the same in the *Pittsburgh Gazette*. In it, they mocked the federal government, which had already begun to assemble troops in case Washington's peacemaking efforts failed. The note read:

Brothers, you must not think to frighten us with fine arranged bits of infantry, cavalry, and artillery, composed of your watermelon armies, taken from the Jersey shores. They would cut a much better figure in warring with crabs and oysters about the banks of the Delaware.

Talk about a saucy taunt. To the president's commissioners, it had become clear that although the western delegates wanted peace, there remained many in the region who refused to back down, who would accept nothing less than a total repeal of the whiskey tax. There was talk of civil war and secession, and it looked as though antigovernment sentiment was spreading to Virginia and Maryland.

Four days earlier than originally planned, on August 28, 1794, the committee members gathered at Redstone Old Fort. When they arrived, they were met by about 70 armed infantrymen parading through the streets beating drums. The next day, when the meeting was called to order, one of the first speakers to address the crowd called for the establishment of an independent government. He went so far as to suggest that those at the meeting should supply themselves with arms and ammunition by attacking the first army sent forth to suppress the insurrection. It was provocative talk, for sure, but few delegates were moved by it, and the floor soon yielded to more moderate speakers.

The time for a vote had come. The resolution: "That in the opinion of this committee, it is in the interest of the people of this country to accede to the proposals made by the Commissioners of the United States." Thirty-four people voted yea. Twenty-three voted nay. It was later learned that those who voted against the resolution did so for fear of retaliation. They'd had enough house burning and enough tarring and feathering, and they saw no reason to set themselves up for more mayhem.

On September 24, having returned to Philadelphia, the commissioners reported in a letter to President Washington the outcome of their meetings with the western representatives. While they at first found the gatherings to be encouraging, their hopes for a peaceful resolution were diminished after the representatives presented the proposed agreements to the people of the counties. The commissioners wanted written promises from individuals that they would submit to the laws, and that violence and intimidation would stop. But few were willing to comply. For this reason, the commissioners recommended that a military force be dispatched to deal with the uprising. The next day, Washington made the official call for federal troops. From Maryland, New Jersey, Pennsylvania, and Virginia came a total of 12,950 men.

On Tuesday, September 30, 1794, at 10:30 in the morning, Washington, accompanied by Secretary of the Treasury Alexander Hamilton, set out from Philadelphia toward the western counties. It was a momentous show of force for the new nation, but one that the President deemed necessary to preserve the union.

Upon reaching Bedford, Pennsylvania, in late October, however, President Washington returned east to Philadelphia, leaving Secretary Hamilton and General Henry Lee, of New Jersey, to forge ahead. On November 9, Lee issued from his headquarters near Parkinson's Ferry a set of instructions and three lists of names. In Allegheny County, the men whose names appeared on the first list were those who had complied with the requests of the president's commissioners, and for that reason were to be left alone. Those on list two were believed to have committed acts of treason and were to be arrested, while men on the third list, witnesses to the events of the insurrection, were also to be apprehended.

Military action commenced in the wee hours of Thursday, November 13, which later came to be known as the "Dreadful Night." At around 2:00 a.m., soldiers raided homes and pulled men from their beds, threatening them with hanging, as children, wives, and mothers watched helplessly. Half-dressed and shoeless, the men were then made to march through cold, muddy streets. Tied back-to-back, they spent the night in barns, stables, and cellars. More than 200 men were arrested. Against Lee's orders, no distinction was made between men who were to be granted amnesty in exchange for their promise to obey the laws and those who were not.

What came next was perhaps even crueler. Twenty men were forced to walk for 30 days to Philadelphia. On Christmas morning, they were paraded, hungry and weak, through the city streets before a boisterous crowd of 20,000, from Blackhorse Tavern to the city jail, each with a white piece of paper stuck in his hat on which the word INSURGENT had been written in big letters.

Ultimately, 12 cases went to trial. But with little evidence, the prosecution fell short, and just two men were convicted, for treason. One of the men, John Mitchell, had robbed the mail in Pittsburgh in an attempt to intercept correspondence sent by the federal government. He was sentenced to death by hanging. Now that peace had been restored, however, President Washington showed mercy on the man, who was generally regarded as mentally challenged, and issued a pardon. The other convicted man was also pardoned.

Looking back, forgiving the whiskey rebels only seemed right, for after serving two terms as president of the United States, and retiring in 1797 to his Virginia farm, Mount Vernon, Washington himself became a distiller. His farm manager, a Scot by the name of James Anderson, had already set up two stills on the property. Over the course of the year, the stills produced more than 600 gallons of whiskey. Washington's "common whiskey" went for around 60 cents a gallon, while the twice-distilled variety sold for about $1 a gallon. Some people paid cash, others bartered, offering in exchange barrels, butter, salt, oysters, candles, and other goods, including grain, which was used to make more whiskey.

Convinced of the distillery's moneymaking potential, Anderson successfully persuaded Washington to grow the operation to five copper pot stills, and to construct near the property's gristmill a new stone building in which to house them. Anderson was the master distiller. To run the operation year-round, he was assisted by his son, John, as manager, and a team of six enslaved distillers.

The endeavor paid off. In 1798, Washington's distillery produced its first batch of clear, unaged whiskey, made from a mash of 60% rye, 35% corn, and 5% malted barley. A year later, the distillery had its greatest output yet: nearly 11,000 gallons of whiskey worth $7,500 at the time, for which Washington paid $332.64 in taxes. Mount Vernon being in a rural area, Washington's distillery was taxed by the capacity of its stills, 616 gallons, not by the actual number of gallons produced, which would have resulted in a heftier bill. Numbers like that made Washington's distillery the country's largest and most prolific. In contrast, other distilleries generally had just one still and produced only a few hundred gallons of liquor a year.

Washington's distillery opened in 1798 and stood until 1814, when it was destroyed in a fire. It reopened in 2007 with the help of a $2.1 million grant from the Distilled Spirits Council of the United

George Washington's Mount Vernon distillery is open for tours.

States, which allowed for the excavation of the site on which it stood and the reconstruction of the two-story stone building. The president paid taxes on his product, so he can't be called a moonshiner. But the product sold today at his distillery offers a taste of the kind of spirit that fueled the Whiskey Rebellion.

Meanwhile, back in western Pennsylvania, whiskey making continued apace, and farmers paid their taxes to government collectors. One of those collectors was General John Neville. Even after his plantation, Bower Hill, was burned to the ground in the violent protest that threatened to undo the new nation, Neville held on to his job as inspector of the revenue. When Congress reimbursed Neville $6,172.88 for the losses he took at Bower Hill, he chose not to rebuild, but to buy land on Montour's Island, in Allegheny County. He remained in the county until his death in 1803, one year after President Thomas Jefferson repealed the whiskey tax. The lawlessness of the Whiskey Rebellion would be followed by decades of peaceful liquor making. The question was, How long could that last?

A TASTE OF HISTORY

Want a taste of Washington's whiskey? At the Mount Vernon estate, in Alexandria, Virginia, the first president's unaged rye sells for $95 a pint. For drinkers desiring a mellower option, Mount Vernon sells for $195 a whiskey aged one year. Both are based on Washington's 200-year-old recipe, and are handcrafted using traditional methods. That means the mash is hand-stirred, then left to ferment in 120-gallon oak barrels. After three weeks, the mash is then transferred to copper pot stills heated by firewood that the still-hands chop themselves. True to the time, everything is done without electricity.

WAR ON WHISKEY TAXING LIQUOR AND DEFYING THE LAW IN THE 1800s

Once two strangers climbed ol' Rocky Top,
Lookin' for a moonshine still.
Strangers ain't come down from Rocky Top,
Reckon they never will.

——Felice and Boudleaux Bryant, "Rocky Top," 1967 (University of
Tennessee's unofficial fight song; recorded by the Osborne Brothers in
1967 and by Lynn Anderson in 1970; and performed 190 times in live
Phish concerts, from 1987 to 2012, according to the fan site Phish.net)

For the better part of the 1800s, the United States government left distillers alone. There was a little blip called the War of 1812, which prompted the feds to once again impose a tax on distilled spirits as a way to finance the effort. But by and large, Washington, D.C., stayed out of the whiskey business.

This was a welcome development, especially for those in Kentucky, where many western Pennsylvanians had resettled in an effort to avoid the upheaval of the Whiskey Rebellion. In the Bluegrass State, corn topped rye as whiskey's main ingredient, and the region's

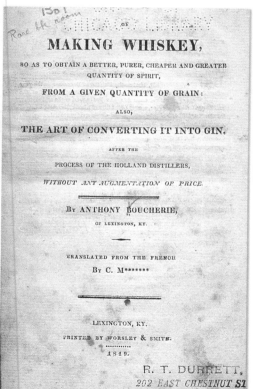

A handbook for distillers, 1819.

crisp, clear limestone creeks provided a desirable water source for mountain distillers. By 1810, Kentucky was home to about 2,000 stills capable of producing more than 2 million gallons of whiskey a year.

Civic-minded individuals sought to pump up profits for Kentucky distillers. One was a French transplant named Anthony Boucherie. In 1819, his ideas were published in a short volume with a lengthy title: *The Art of Making Whiskey, So As to Obtain a Better, Purer, Cheaper, and Greater Quantity of Spirit, from a Given Quantity of Grain.*

Boucherie's treatise pointed to whiskey's role in American culture. "The most usual drink in the United States, is whiskey," he wrote. "Other spirituous liquors, such as peach and apple brandy, are only secondary, and from their high price and their scarcity, they are not sufficient for the wants of an already immense and increasing population."

Boucherie professed as his goal a desire to perfect the "art of whiskey making" and "to contribute to the welfare of the United States, and even to the health of the American, and to the prosperity of the distiller. . . ."

Four years later, an unnamed author delivered at the Kentucky Institute, in Lexington, an oration on a similar theme: "An Essay on the Importance and the Best Mode of Converting Grain into Spirit, as a Means of Promoting the Wealth and Prosperity of the Western Country." Included in the essay were whiskey-making instructions. To contemporary readers, the tips sound as if they were intended for vampires and sadists. "More water is then added of the warmth of human blood," the writer explains in a section about how to malt grain. And later, in a recipe: "Let it stand until so cool that the distiller can bear his hand four inches within the surface of the mash, without more pain than a slight stinging sensation at the ends of his fingers."

Any increase in profit for distillers as a result of these efforts, however, would soon be blunted. The U.S. government, in need of cash to finance the Civil War, turned once again to taxation, and on

ALL-AMERICAN WHISKEY

Bourbon was born in Kentucky. It's whiskey, but as the saying goes, "All bourbon is whiskey, but not all whiskey is bourbon." So what sets bourbon apart? It must be made in the United States, from at least 51% corn. In addition, it must be aged in new, charred oak barrels and distilled at no more than 160 proof, or 80% alcohol by volume. It's stored at no more than 125 proof, or about 62% alcohol by volume. The liquor gets its name from Bourbon County, though it doesn't have to be made there to claim the name. But back in the day, the county name was stamped on the barrels used to store the whiskey, and when shipments of it arrived in New Orleans after a long trip down the Mississippi and Ohio Rivers, drinkers enjoyed the flavor of the aged spirit, and they took to calling it bourbon because of that stamp. In 1964, Congress officially designated bourbon as a product indigenous to the United States. Distillers proudly call it America's Native Spirit.

In 1999, the Kentucky Distillers Association established the Kentucky Bourbon Trail as a way to introduce tourists to seven of the country's oldest distilleries, including Maker's Mark, in Loretto, which dates back to 1805, and Jim Beam, in Clermont, with a distilling tradition that began in 1795. The other distilleries on the trail are Wild Turkey, Four Roses, Woodford Reserve, Town Branch, and Heaven Hill. In the past five years, the Kentucky Bourbon Trail has attracted more than 2.5 million visitors.

August 5, 1861, President Abraham Lincoln created the nation's first federal income tax. (It would later be repealed, then reinstated in 1913 in a modified form with the ratification of the 16th Amendment.) In addition to collecting a percentage of an individual's personal income, the government also benefited by imposing a sales tax on items as diverse as brass, calfskins, candles, furs, parasols, pickles, preserved meats, silk, varnish, wood, and wool. Additionally, the law called for a flat tax on certain professions. Architects, confectioners,

"'The Moonshine Man' of Kentucky," *Harper's Weekly*, October 20, 1877.

dentists, lawyers, soap makers, and surgeons paid $10. Jugglers paid $20, and distillers of spirituous liquor paid a maximum flat tax of $50 and a per-gallon tax of 20 cents. The taxes, of course, were paid only in Union states, as the law allowing for their collection went into effect in 1862, one year after the Civil War began.

In his 1863 report for the Bureau of Internal Revenue—the first report since the tax was instituted—commissioner Joseph J. Lewis recommended that the tax on spirits be raised from 20 cents to $1 per gallon, noting that the rate was far less than the one levied on distilled spirits in Great Britain. An equivalent sum in the U.S., he warned, would be tough to enforce and hard to collect. He wrote, "With our long frontier, and the vast tracts of land in our northwestern States, sparsely settled and remote from the observation of the government and its officers, there would be very great difficulty in preventing and punishing smuggling and illicit distillation were our tax rate on spirits made as heavy as is the English." He went on to say that if the government were to institute a steeper tax, it would be "perpetually at war."

Lewis's prediction turned out to be true. Within the space of a single year, 1864, the federal liquor tax went from 20 cents to 60 cents to $1.50 a gallon. After the end of the Civil War, between 1865 and 1868, the tax on whiskey and other spirits climbed to $2 a gallon. The steep tax would lead to an outbreak of illicit distilling. And it wasn't confined to rural areas or to the South, which now provided for the government an expanded tax-collection region. City people were making whiskey, and it was in cities and in immigrant neighborhoods where law enforcement agents focused a considerable amount of effort.

"Since the 1st of January last, when the law making the duty two dollars per gallon went into effect, the number of stills of every conceivable capacity that have been put into operation is absolutely incredible," noted the *New York Times*, in an article dated May 24, 1865. "Wherever you find a German or Irish drinking-shop, ten to one, the inspection of the cellar, kitchen, or some part of the establishment, will show you a still at work, converting molasses,

HARPER'S WEEKLY.

ILLICIT DISTILLATION OF LIQUORS—HOW THE ARTICLE IS CARRIED TO THE SOUTHERN MARKETS.—[SKETCHED BY A. W. THOMPSON.]

ILLICIT DISTILLATION OF LIQUORS.

MANY of the methods employed by the army speculators who are defrauding the Govern-

the Lower Bay, and the whisky thus made is smuggled into the city.

This method of defrauding the Government is very largely practiced at the South. In some of the mountain regions of the Southern States this

ists. The liquor is stored in kegs, and carried down the mountains on sleds; as there are no roads the use of vehicles on those rough trails is unknown. One would suppose that the spirits so manufactured would be of a good quality (as

is a remedy for some diseases. Of late our parties have been arrested for smuggling in Western North Carolina, as detachments of cavalry are continually on the look-out for them. The engravings on this page illustrate one of the mountain stills in operation, and the manner

"Illicit distillation of liquors—how the article is carried to the southern markets," *Harper's Weekly*, December 7, 1867.

sour beer, or something that can be used, and which can be bought cheap, and quietly smuggled into the premises, into spirits, which are as quietly put on the market, at such low prices, that even the purchaser finds it to his interest to keep quiet and such as utterly astonishes the legitimate operator."

Raids by revenue agents hired to enforce the tax law often turned violent. In Philadelphia, in the fall of 1867, 12 agents descended upon Port Richmond. Located along the Delaware River, the neighborhood was home to Irish laborers, many of whom worked at the port unloading wheelbarrows of black coal brought into the city by rail from mines in the state's northeastern region. A shot of whiskey was a fine reward for hours of strenuous work on the docks, and thirsty neighbors turned Richmond into a hotbed of illegal distilling.

The raid was a dubious endeavor. After arriving in the neighborhood at midday, the agents succeeded in disrupting illicit distillers and loading their horse-drawn wagons with copper stills and other confiscated equipment. But news of the seizure traveled quickly, and as they made their way down Salmon Street, the officers were swarmed by an angry mob of between 200 and 300 men, women, and children. The rioters shouted insults and threats and pelted the agents with stones. One man beat an officer with a club, but was subdued when his victim managed to fire at him with a revolver. Then, in the midst of the fray, two women broke through the crowd and repossessed a still from the agents' haul. A report in the *Philadelphia Bulletin* described one of them as an "Amazon, more athletic and bold than the rest." With six of their men seriously wounded, the agents were forced to retreat, and to leave behind the material they'd attempted to cart away.

In response to such violent opposition, the federal government eventually backed down, and in 1868 lowered the tax on spirits from $2 to 50 cents per gallon. Yet even with the tax decrease, the cat-and-mouse game continued. Distillers kept on conducting their covert businesses, and federal agents kept going after them. In Brooklyn, New York, the feds staged a massive effort on Friday, December 3, 1869, assembling at the Brooklyn Navy Yard a group of more than 500 soldiers, war veterans, and Internal Revenue officers. In the predawn hours, the men formed a column, and marched beyond the naval compound's main gates at Sands Street into the neighborhood known as Irishtown (now called Vinegar Hill). Their goals: bust up distilleries; confiscate whiskey.

The men were better prepared than their Philadelphia counterparts. Sheer numbers gave them a decided advantage. With rifles, axes, and crowbars at the ready, they fanned out in different directions. Residents, who were likely busy cooking breakfast, threw open their windows and popped their heads out into the cold morning air to see what all the commotion was about. It must have been a shock to see an army convened on the cobblestone streets, and the sight surely sent many people scrambling to their stills to save what whiskey they could.

The soldiers' attack was unforgiving, and so was the reaction of the locals. At a distillery set up in the center of an open lot ringed by shanties, government men began smashing stills. Hot whiskey flowed into the streets. Witnesses cursed the soldiers and threatened violence against them. But there was little they could do to stop the destruction.

Searching the neighborhood, soldiers beat down walls and ripped up floors, leaving jagged piles of splintered timber in their wake. In a sizable wooden shed on Little Street, they captured the day's biggest prize: thousands of gallons of whiskey in wooden casks arranged beneath a warm still.

As the troops marched south on Little Street on their way back to the Navy Yard, they were met on Plymouth Street with a hail of bricks and stones hurled from rooftops and windows. At least one soldier was hit in the head with a flying object. Another suffered a broken nose, causing blood to burst from his face.

BRINGING DISTILLING BACK TO BROOKLYN

More than 140 years after the government's assault on whiskey makers in Brooklyn's Irishtown, distilling has made a comeback in the borough. Kings County Distillery was the first to open in Brooklyn since Prohibition. Founded in 2010, it's located at the Brooklyn Navy Yard, just inside the Sands Street gate where revenue agents assembled, ready to raid, in 1869. Also in Brooklyn, along the waterfront in the borough's Red Hook neighborhood, is Van Brunt Stillhouse, maker of moonshine, whiskey, rum, and grappa. In Williamsburg, there's New York Distilling Company, cofounded by Tom Potter, who in 1987 was part of a team that started Brooklyn Brewery. These three businesses are among 10 distilleries and a wine shop that make up the Brooklyn Spirits Trail, an urban microdistiller's riff on the Kentucky Bourbon Trail.

"Close up!" one of the commanders called out as he saw the threat worsening. Officers flashed their revolvers and retreated to the Navy Yard. By 12:30 that afternoon, the operation was over. In all, 13 distilleries had been destroyed, and copper stills and other equipment needed for distilling, along with 35 barrels of whiskey, were stored in the compound.

With the troops gone, a group of men coalesced on Little and Plymouth Streets. Cheered on by the crowd, a man by the name of Dennis Muldoon climbed atop a whiskey barrel and addressed his neighbors. A reporter for the *Brooklyn Eagle* observed the speechifying. He transcribed it, in dialect, and reported it in the day's newspaper:

> Here ye seed to-day a lot of fellers because they had blue coats on and white badges, come and rob decent white min of their whiskey. What right has dey to steal whiskey from us. If we go steal of whiskey, we gets sent up. Cos why? Cos we're poor. But these fellers cos theys 'pinted by President Grant they can steal any think. . . . Is this civil guvening, when a dirty lot av blackguards wid goold lace and swords and drums and muskets, can come in and steal a poor man's whisky. Av course it isn't. . . . Now lets take a drink, and may bad luck follow the dirty divils.

It was the people of Irishtown, however, who were met with bad luck. Nearly one year later, their neighborhood was again teeming with federal troops. This time, there were 2,000 of them. Wrote the *Brooklyn Eagle*:

> We have seen detectives go into this whiskey district not worth a dollar, and in a few months emerge with enormous fortunes. We see notice given in public print of men whom the officials know to be carrying on illicit whiskey-making,

"Law and moonshine—crooked whiskey in North Carolina," *Harper's Weekly*, August 3, 1873.

and then no seizure or arrest, only a private settlement between the detected offender and the superserviceable detective. . . . Thus whiskey tax evasion in the Fifth Ward is contemporaneous with fortune, fame and ambition, among the Federal officials. The illicit whiskey trade thrives apace; and the Federal officials get rich by vaporing about it and making pompous pretences of stopping it.

Eagle editors were keen observers; prescient, too. Whiskey-tax evasion reached far beyond Brooklyn, and was spectacular in its scope. In 1874, newly appointed Secretary of the Treasury Benjamin H. Bristow began a secret investigation into a conspiracy by distillers and revenue agents to defraud the federal government of tax dollars by reporting only a portion of actual liquor sales and splitting the money amongst themselves. The illegal activity, which went on primarily in St. Louis, Milwaukee, and Chicago, became known as the Whiskey Ring. A St. Louis grand jury in 1875 indicted 238 individuals, including General Orville E. Babcock, personal secretary to President Ulysses S. Grant. Ultimately, Babcock was acquitted, but only after a deposition from the president himself was admitted into evidence; 110 people were convicted; and more than $3 million in unpaid revenue was recovered.

Meanwhile, illicit distilling had reached epidemic proportions in the South. In his 1877 report, Internal Revenue Commissioner Green B. Raum raised the alarm about the subterfuge and law-evading that his agents saw unfolding in several states, including Georgia, Kentucky, North Carolina, Tennessee, and West Virginia:

The extent of these frauds would startle belief. I can safely say that during the past year not less than three thousand illicit stills have been operated in the districts named. These stills are of a producing capacity of from ten to fifty gallons per day. They are usually located at inaccessible points in the mountains, away from ordinary lines of travel, and are generally owned by unlettered men of desperate character, armed and ready to resist officers of the law. When occasion requires, they come together in companies of from ten to fifty persons, gun in hand, to drive the officers out of the country. They resist as long as resistance is possible, and when their stills are seized and they themselves are arrested, they plead ignorance and poverty, and at once crave the pardon of the government.

The disastrous results of the Civil War were seen as one reason for southerners' deep antigovernment sentiment. Many southern moonshiners thought the whiskey tax to be particularly odious, imposed, as it had been, as a way to fund the war. Not only that, but many people saw the tax as an unfair burden on the region's poor. Why, they asked, should struggling farmers be prevented from turning their grain into whiskey, a far more profitable product? Whiskey making was a means of subsistence for mountain folk, a time-honored, traditional way to support a family, and many observers saw the government's response to illicit distilling as disproportionate to the problem. An 1878 article in the *New York Times* summed up the view of local leaders: "It is like, they say, putting up a steam-hammer to stamp out a few potato-bugs."

Just as they had in Pennsylvania during the Whiskey Rebellion, moonshiners in the South fought back against the collectors, banding together to wage vicious attacks against those who dared cross into their territory. In 1877, a team of 11 revenue agents in Overton County, Tennessee, after traveling for three days on foot on the trail of local moonshiners, stopped for the evening at a farmhouse. That night, armed men circled the property. They fired upon the officers, and as the hours wore on, more aggressors joined the mob until their number swelled to 200. The officers took shelter in a log house, and the siege continued for 42 hours. In the end, 3 of the 11 agents had been shot. Whether or not the moonshiners suffered casualties is unknown.

The 1879 Internal Revenue Commissioner's report showed that in the span of three years, government agents seized 3,117 illicit distilleries and arrested 6,431 distillers. Also during that period, the report noted that 26 revenue agents were killed and 47 wounded. There were more battles to come. In 1880, a deputy and his assistant in Georgia came face-to-face with 12 angry men. One of them fired on the assistant, and the shot grazed the man's scalp, the gunpowder burning his hair and whiskers. The deputy succeeded in capturing one prisoner, whom he subdued with a pistol whipping.

Violence continued. On the night of April 25, 1886, in Manchester, Tennessee, a band of masked men broke into the home of D.W. Purdam, whom they believed to be a government informant. With his wife and children nearby, the men shot at Purdam, hitting him in the arm and on the left side of his body. Another shot lodged in the mattress, setting it on fire. Purdam rallied well enough to reach for his revolver and shoot one of the assailants, who fell to the floor. The intruder, who was dressed in a Ku Klux Klan costume, was later identified as a legal distiller. However, he was thought to also be involved in the production of "crooked whiskey" and seeking retribution against Purdam.

Plenty of southerners were either afraid of moonshiners or sympathized with them. Many also shared the moonshiner's deep hatred for government agents. In his 1877 report, Commissioner Raum offered two cases in point. The first concerned a revenuer searching for a still in South Carolina's Blue Ridge Mountains. On his rounds, he was ambushed by gunfire and instantly killed, leaving behind a wife and baby. "This deed scarcely created a ripple on the surface of the public mind," Raum noted.

In contrast, Raum told the story of three government agents, also in South Carolina, who killed a notorious moonshiner who was resisting arrest. The agents were subsequently jailed, held without bail, and convicted in a local court, the judge refusing to turn over the men's cases to the U.S. Circuit Court.

Revenue agent George W. Atkinson wrote about the illicit whiskey trade in his 1881 book *After the Moonshiners, By One of the Raiders*. He detailed the experiences of tax collectors in Appalachia, on the trail of moonshiners who set up their stills in the region's cliffs, caves, and hollows. To find moonshiners, some revenuers went undercover as hunters and fishermen, or traveling salesmen peddling clocks and tin. It gave them an excuse for poking around in the heavily wooded hills where moonshine operations were hidden far off the main roads.

Agents developed sharp senses to track their prey. They sniffed out the telltale scent of sour, fermenting corn, and learned to identify bubbles in a stream as a signal that distillers must be close by. The bubbles meant the water was laced with corn mash, so agents simply moved upstream to find the offenders. In at least one instance, animal tracks led agents to a still. Officers assigned to Pulaski County, Kentucky, followed the footprints of sheep, which brought them to a still set up in the entrance to a cave and concealed by bushes and overhanging trees. The sheep, it seems, enjoyed eating corn slop left over from the distillation process.

Atkinson also profiled in his book legendary collectors, esteemed for their bravery, skill, and compassionate approach in a dangerous profession. One of them was then-33-year-old James M. Davis, of Tennessee:

> He is six foot two and one-half inches tall; is large boned, and muscular, and tips the beam at two hundred and ten pounds avoirdupois. Although of great courage, and physical strength and endurance, he is one of the kindest hearted and most gentle natured of men. The individuals against whom he has operated for violations of the law quake at the bare mention of his name; and yet, when he has made an

arrest, he never fails to win the affection of the prisoner. He has arrested upwards of three thousand violators of the law, and I am credibly informed there is scarcely one of this vast number of wrong doers, who would not divide his last dime and morsel with Davis; and, if necessary, would even shed his blood in his defence.

Other agents, too, had a soft spot for the men they pursued. In 1898, one revenuer working in Georgia found a creative way to engage the moonshiners' talents and steer them toward reputable employment, persuading an Atlanta judge to release a group of men from jail on the condition that they enlist in the army. As one newspaper article explained, "They will join the company of moonshiners being organized here by Capt. Yancey Carter, the noted revenue officer, who says they are especially adapted to guerilla warfare."

The military wasn't an option for women moonshiners. Fifty-year-old Melinda Turner was arrested at her one-room, hillside home in rural White County, Georgia, in 1893, and locked up in an Atlanta jail. She pleaded guilty. "I have made whisky since my old man died," she said, "and I guess I'll make it till I go whar he is. I got as good a still as anybody right there on the crick, and I'm as good a hand to make the corn juice as you ever laid eyes on in your borned days. I used ter make four runs a day, and nights I'd double up. By myself? Well, I guess thar waren't nobody 'sides me, and I had to do it all."

Another woman liquor maker, from Warren County, New Jersey, was known only by the nickname "Crazy Nancy." A decade after her double life was revealed, a newspaper writer dubbed her "Nancy the Moonshiner."

The year was 1886. Thought to be eccentric and dim, Nancy nonetheless appeared well-versed in the ways of finance, selling berries and game at local markets and exhibiting the ability to drive a hard bargain. Over time, locals came to suspect Nancy of distilling applejack, or "Jersey lightning," the state's popular spirit, using apples stolen from nearby orchards. A government detective was assigned to stake her out, and for two months, he worked undercover on a farm near Nancy's humble dwelling, which stood on a bluff near the Pequest River. At night, he concealed himself in the bushes to observe her comings and goings.

One evening, the detective saw at Nancy's doorstep a man carrying over his shoulder a large sack. That explained the missing apples, the detective thought. But it also raised a question: Who was this mysterious man? The detective never guessed that Crazy Nancy would have friends or associates.

A week went by. Seeing Nancy leave the property, the detective decided that he needed to have a look inside. He picked the lock and let himself in. The home was sparsely furnished. A string of dried apples hung near the fireplace. In the corner, the detective spotted a ladder leading to an open hatch in the ceiling. He climbed into the loft. Finding nothing unusual inside, he hid behind a barrel of flour until Nancy returned. Through the floorboards, he could see into her kitchen.

Two hours later, Nancy came back. She fixed herself a meal, and an hour after that, lit a candle, locked the front door, and made her way to the loft. From his hiding place, the detective saw Nancy open a small door in the back of the room and enter a chamber dug into the side of the cliff. In 30 minutes, a man emerged. By candlelight, the detective could see that it was Nancy dressed in men's clothing. She was carrying a sack, and the detective concluded that she was going out to steal apples.

While Nancy was thieving fruit, the detective inspected the mysterious room carved into the mountain. It was home to Nancy's moonshine operation, complete with a still, 50 large jugs, and more apples than the detective could count. On the floor was a pile of women's clothes. The detective went back downstairs and waited in the kitchen.

It was midnight before Crazy Nancy returned. She walked in and plunked down a sack of apples on the floor. The detective made his move. "Hold up your hands," he said, while aiming his revolver at Nancy. Nancy, holding a candle, immediately blew it out. She reached for a stool and swung it, knocking the detective down. Before he could get up, Nancy was off. She was not apprehended.

The next day, a search of the property turned up 500 gallons of applejack stored in jugs under the floorboards and in the cavern. Authorities determined that Crazy Nancy probably concealed her product in barrels of animal hides, walnuts, and chestnuts that she transported by rail to Philadelphia and New York.

Like thousands of other small-scale distillers across the country, Crazy Nancy had found in moonshining a reliable source of income, and a way to evade and fight back against government agents who would come after her livelihood.

In his 1913 book *Our Southern Highlanders*, Horace Kephart summed up the moonshiner's economic motivation. "Men do not make whiskey in secret, at the peril of imprisonment or death, because they are outlaws by nature nor from any other kind of depravity, but simply and solely because it looks like 'easy money to poor folks.'"

In the space of a century, whiskey making had gone from being the respectable subject of lectures and essays aimed at boosting American agriculture and entrepreneurship to an underground endeavor fueled by poverty and marked by deception and violence, the worst of which was yet to come.

PROHIBITION'S RISE AND FALL, AND WHAT HAPPENED IN BETWEEN

Well, you want a little drink I'll meet you on the hill.
Your head'll start spinning and you can't sit still.
Your eyes are turning greener than a $20 bill.
You know you been drinkin' from an 80-gallon still.
Moonshine, moonshine. Oh, yeah, if you drink that
    stuff you're bound to go blind.

—Jack Holt, "Moonshine Still," 1963
(released by Chuck Garner Records, East Point, Georgia)

In an illustrated, four-panel broadside titled *The Drunkard's Progress, or The Direct Road to Poverty, Wretchedness & Ruin*, published in 1826, a husband reaches for a bottle stored in a kitchen cabinet. The caption sums up the scene: "The Beginning of Sorrow, Neglect of Business, Languor, Loss of Appetite, Dullness and Heaviness, a Love of Strong Drink Increasing." The panels that follow show the man's worsening condition. In "The Grog Shop," he spews vomit while a fistfight breaks out beside him. "The Confirmed Drunkard" shows him at home again, this time on the floor, alongside a knocked-over chair, distressed children, and sobbing wife. In the final scene, the family is loaded up in a wagon on its way to the almshouse.

America's heavy drinking habit and nascent temperance movement were behind the editorializing. As they did during Colonial times, American drinkers in the early 1800s imbibed throughout the day: nip in the morning, a glass of beer in the afternoon while on a break from working the fields, another at the end of the day, and a tipple to send them off to sleep. And the drinks

The Drunkard's Progress, by John Warner Barber, 1826.

kept coming. Twenty years after the original *Drunkard's Progress*, lithographer Nathanial Currier created his own version of the anti-alcohol propaganda. His featured nine steps along an arched wall, a distillery in the distance, and a harrowing sequence that ends with a man shooting himself in the head.

When it came to alcohol, the country was at a crisis point. In 1850, Maine became the first state to ban the manufacture and sale of intoxicating beverages. Protests led to the law's repeal in 1856, but in 1885, prohibition would become part of the state's constitution.

The temperance movement saw significant growth in the latter part of the nineteenth century. In Hillsboro, Ohio, on Christmas Eve, 1873, a group of 70 mothers, sisters, wives, and daughters, led by Eliza Jane Trimble Thompson, marched from the First

"The Ohio Whiskey War—the ladies of Logan singing hymns in front of barrooms in aid of the temperance movement," from *Frank Leslie's Illustrated Newspaper*, February 21, 1874.

Presbyterian Church to a local drinking establishment. There, in a daring act of civil disobedience, they kneeled on the snowy sidewalk, blocked the doorway, uttered prayers, and sang a hymn, "Give to the Winds Thy Fears." They called their movement the Women's Crusade, and succeeded in their efforts to shut down or stop the sale of intoxicating liquors in Hillsboro's 21 hotels, drugstores, and saloons, including a "low-down," sawdust-on-the-floor tavern called the Lava Bed.

One year later, the Women's Christian Temperance Union (WCTU) was founded in Cleveland, Ohio. Its leader was Frances Willard, a handsome woman with rimless glasses, hair severely parted down the middle, and the self-given nickname "Frank." Under Willard, the WCTU made total abstinence its mission, organizing a public health campaign that included the installation of outdoor drinking fountains to provide a healthful alternative to alcohol for men tempted by saloons, and a curriculum called Scientific Temperance Instruction. By 1901, the group had succeeded in making its teachings mandatory in the nation's public schools. Their message to young people: Alcohol is poison; just one sip can lead to addiction. In rare cases, they said, it could even result in spontaneous human combustion.

Meanwhile, in Kansas, a nearly six-foot-tall, 175-pound woman named Carrie Nation brought an even more radical edge to the temperance movement. In 1900, she traveled 25 miles from her home in Medicine Lodge to Kiowa, where she used rocks to smash up saloons. She later explained that God had called her to Kiowa to stamp out the demon drink. After all, Nation told authorities, if the state would not enforce its own Constitutional amendment against alcohol, ratified in 1880, she would do the job for them. Who was to stop her, since all she was doing was targeting establishments that weren't legal in the first place? Nation went on to destroy saloons throughout the state, using as her tool of choice a hatchet, with which she would become forever associated.

The heaviest hitter in the crusade against alcohol, however, was the Anti-Saloon League (ASL), founded in Oberlin, Ohio, in 1893. Led by Wayne B. Wheeler, the ASL first pushed for local and state laws against alcohol, then federal legislation. The group's pressure tactics bore fruit. By the early part of the 1900s, one state after the next went dry. Georgia and Oklahoma did so first, in 1907, the latter writing prohibition into the new state's constitution. In 1908, statewide prohibition came to Mississippi and North Carolina. Tennessee passed its law against alcohol in 1909, followed by West Virginia in 1914. Alabama went dry the following year, and Virginia passed its law in 1916. By 1917, prohibition was the law of the land in 26 states. A resolution calling for a national ban on alcohol had been introduced in Congress.

It was a popular proposal. On January 16, 1919, 36 states ratified the 18th Amendment, which would make it against U.S. law to manufacture, sell, or transport intoxicating beverages. Ten more states followed; Connecticut and Rhode Island declined to ratify. The National Prohibition Act, or Volstead Act, named after its author, Minnesota representative Andrew Volstead, would provide a means by which to enforce the new law, defining *intoxicating liquors* as any drink with an alcohol content above 0.5%. Exactly one year after ratification, at 12:01 a.m. (EST), on January 16, 1920, the United States officially went dry.

To mark the occasion, former National League Baseball player turned influential evangelist William "Billy" Sunday led a mock funeral for "John Barleycorn"—a folk name for beer and whiskey—in front of 10,000 "mourners" in Norfolk, Virginia. A dispatch from the event ran in the *New York Times*. It reported that the procession began at a railroad station, where the corpse, in a 20-foot-long coffin, was unloaded from a train then marched through the streets by 20 pallbearers. Bringing up the rear was "His Satanic Majesty," anguished, as the cortege made its way to Sunday's tabernacle.

Police officers in Washington, D.C., pose with confiscated moonshine, 1922.

"Good-bye, John," Sunday said at the close of his sermon. "You were God's worst enemy; you were Hell's best friend. I hate you with a perfect hatred; I love to hate you."

For all of Sunday's passionate distaste, there were countless others for whom the alcohol ban only worked to increase their thirst. In New York and Chicago and other big cities, the well-to-do, the well-known, and the well-connected consumed alcohol in nightclubs, and tucked-away speakeasies, to which men and women gained admittance after identifying themselves with a special rap on the door and a whispered password to prove they weren't agents of the law. In small towns, the speakeasy was often a drugstore, poolroom, or gas station, with patrons drinking right out in the open. At a Pittsburgh soda fountain, "white moonshine whisky," "colored moonshine whisky," and gin flowed from the spigots. In Washington, D.C., bootleggers not only sold illegal liquor to the very members of Congress who voted for national prohibition, but they supplied top-shelf whiskey to President Warren G. Harding's White House.

A DEADLY DRINK

When a 28-year-old farmer was admitted to a Virginia hospital complaining of severe stomach cramps, nausea, and vomiting, in 1921, doctors didn't know what was wrong. Questioning of the patient revealed that the man was a heavy drinker, consuming each day as much as one quart of homemade whiskey. As it turned out, his still's worm—the coiled portion of the rig where alcohol-heavy steam is condensed into liquid—was made from lead pipe. It was not an isolated incident, this young farmer's bout with lead poisoning. Drinkers across the United States were similarly afflicted.

Much of the booze flowed into the United States from Canada, smuggled across the border by bootleggers in airplanes, automobiles, trains, and ships, which anchored in international waters up and down the East and West coasts. Smaller boats ferried Canadian whiskey and West Indian rum from the Bahamas to Florida.

But smuggling was just part of the picture. One way unscrupulous entrepreneurs satisfied America's demand for liquor was with denatured alcohol, which they diverted from legitimate use as an ingredient in fuels, cleaning solvents, insecticides, explosives, and other toxic substances, redistilling it in an effort to wash away the poisonous methanol, or wood alcohol, that had been added by the government to make it undrinkable. Then they mixed it with legitimate spirits—just one more way to stretch the yield and make a profit. Unfortunately, denatured alcohol really was as dangerous as the government made it out to be, and simply washing away the bad stuff didn't work.

Moonshine poisoning occurred in other ways, too. In the old days, shiners took care to discard the "heads and tails" of a run of whiskey. These first and last runs in the distillation process contained acetaldehyde and fusel oil, the dangerous byproducts of the distillation process. A 1923 editorial titled "The Menace of 'Moonshine' Whisky," in the *Journal of the American Medical Association*, described the "evident stupefying or knockout effects of this liquor."

Stories of casualties came in from across the country. In New Jersey, in 1922, whiskey tainted with wood alcohol led, in a little less than a month's time, to blindness and death for 27 people, including a father and son and the man who sold it to them. During the holiday season that same year, "poisonous Christmas liquor" was responsible for 9 deaths in New York City, one death and 23 illnesses in Detroit, and one death and 2 blindings in Shelby, Ohio, where the men who made the deadly hooch were forced to stand for five minutes before the coffin of the deceased and "gaze upon the body . . . as a moral example."

A year later, one man was found dead in a bog in La Grange Park, Illinois, a suburb of Chicago, after a night of drinking 15-cent shots with three friends at a local saloon. The proprietress, a 34-year-old Polish immigrant and mother of three, Mary Wazeniak, was convicted of manslaughter and sent to the penitentiary in Joliet, the first woman to be sentenced under Illinois state law for selling poisoned liquor. Prosecutors contended that the moon she made and sold was laced with wood alcohol. Wazeniak's sentence: one year to life. The press dubbed her "Moonshine Mary."

Deaths linked to "coroner's cocktails" drew outrage from anti-Prohibition forces. But year after year, the deaths kept coming. In New York City, on New Year's Eve, 1926, the health department reported that the yearly death toll from poison alcohol had reached 750. In 1930, 24 people died in less than a month, prompting medical examiner Dr. Charles Norris to declare an epidemic, saying, "A flood of poison liquor is sweeping the city."

A man inspects a moonshine still in El Paso, Texas, 1920s.

Agents in San Francisco dismantle a still (date unknown).

It was moonshiners, not smugglers of legitimate alcohol from outside the country or diverters of industrial alcohol, who provided the bulk of illicit liquor during Prohibition. In the South, illegal production skyrocketed, as did prices. White whiskey, which once sold for $2 a gallon, tops, could now command $22. One had only to look at the statistics to understand the scope of the problem. Prior to Prohibition, in 1913, the commissioner of the Internal Revenue reported that federal agents had seized 2,375 stills. But by 1929, nearly a decade into what President Herbert Hoover called the nation's "Noble Experiment," it was reported that one state alone had confiscated "more than this number and the federal government half as many more." To put it another way, the combined seizure of stills by state and federal agents in 1929 was 12 times the number of seizures in 1913.

During Prohibition, places and people not normally associated with moonshining were making headlines. In Boston, an assistant professor at Harvard Medical School was found to be operating an "elaborate still" in his Back Bay apartment, his product allegedly served at "dances and other social affairs." On the other side of the country, Prohibition agents in Los Angeles heard outside a five-

DOUBLE TROUBLE

City moonshiners found crafty ways to transport their goods. In Milwaukee, in the summer of 1921, a pair of deputy sheriffs on the lookout for Prohibition violators stopped to talk with a woman taking her children out for a stroll. One of the kids was a 4-year-old girl; the other, a baby in a carriage. When the officers asked to see the little one, the mother refused. She told the men that the child was sick. The agents' interest now piqued, they persisted, and when they pulled back the blanket found not a baby but "twins"—"two two-gallon jugs of moonshine."

room ranch house a sound "like the roar of surf." Upon entering the dwelling, they found a 250-gallon still, 60 gallons of kerosene used to heat it, and four large vats, each containing 800 gallons of mash for making whiskey. Agents in nearby Alhambra, California, also made a surprising discovery: a 10-year-old boy in charge of a 50-gallon still. When questioned, the "Baby Moonshiner" told officers that his father had taught him how to do the job. His parents were arrested when they pulled in the driveway.

Further up the coast, moonshiners in San Francisco were turning out "jackass brandy," made from fruit, and in Oregon's Multnomah County, which includes Portland, 15 stills used to make corn whiskey were raided in a single month in 1926. The *New York Times* reported that in Washington State, "the ancient ways of the Tennessee and Kentucky mountaineers are being imitated in the vast forest lands, where moonshining has become a highly perfected industry."

Another place where moonshining had become a highly perfected industry was Chicago, home to mob boss "Scarface" Al Capone. His

DIRTY DISTILLING

Many moonshiners back in the day would not have scored well with health inspectors. Describing the questionable places where his agents had uncovered stills, Prohibition Commissioner Roy A. Haynes in 1923 told of cringe-worthy sanitary conditions. "Air, sunlight, and pure water cannot be had in the dark basements, stables, holes in the ground, cellars, and attics—nor even in the remote thickets—where moonshine is made," he wrote. "Snakes, mice, rats, and even cats have been found in vats," he continued. "They were not deliberately put there; they fell in and were drowned, and the moonshiner either did not know it at the time or did not take the trouble to remove them."

name turned up in connection with a massive sting operation that resulted in 50 raids yielding 320 arrests, 10,000 barrels of mash, another 10,000 gallons of alcohol, and a cache of shotguns, revolvers, and knives. The investigation revealed that hundreds of stills were operated at locations throughout the city by Italian immigrants, many of whom came from Sicily, at the behest of the Genna crime family. Newspaper photographs show uniformed police officers posing on top of drums of alcohol seized on Taylor Street, in Chicago's Little Italy, and piles of stills ("new ones and old ones, big ones and little ones") that had been ripped out of the city's "booze dens" by police.

America's hill country had crime bosses, too. The way it worked was simple: A big-time operator would hire local moonshiners to make a few gallons of whiskey at a time. He'd also set up larger, clandestine plants, to guarantee a bigger, faster output. Product was then picked up by drivers who transported the moonshine to bigger markets. If a still was busted by the feds, the benefactor quickly replaced it. He also took care of lawyer fees when it came time for a man to face the law. And if that man was sent to prison—and many a man was—the boss would make sure the man's family was taken care of financially. Upon his release, the man was guaranteed a place back at the still.

As Prohibition wore on, it became all too apparent that the government's attempt to control the social habits of the country's more than 122 million people just might not be working out as planned. The irony was almost too great: A law that promised to improve Americans' health and morals led to deaths by poisoned liquor and flagrant criminality.

Was repeal an option? In 1929, President Herbert Hoover decided it was time to find out, charging a 10-member commission with a daunting task: "A thorough inquiry into the problem of the enforcement of prohibition under the provisions of the Eighteenth Amendment of the Constitution and laws enacted in pursuance thereof, together with the enforcement of other laws."

When it was released two years later, in January 1931, the report by the National Commission on Law Observance and Enforcement, or the Wickersham Commission (for its head, former U.S. attorney general George W. Wickersham), caused a stir, not only because of the corruption, abuse of power, and utter senselessness it revealed, but also for its confounding conclusion that the 18th Amendment should remain in place and that there should be no modification of the Volstead Act.

In his column for the *New York World*, poet Franklin Pierce Adams famously mocked the report:

Prohibition is an awful flop.

We like it.

It can't stop what it's meant to stop.

We like it.

It's left a trail of graft and slime,

It don't prohibit worth a dime,

It's filled our land with vice and crime.

Nevertheless, we're for it.

And there was something else. Addendums to the Wickersham Commission report pointed a finger at Virginia's southwestern Blue Ridge Mountain region, an area long associated with moonshine production. It read, "In one county (Franklin) it is claimed that 99 out of 100 people are making, or have some connection with, illicit liquor."

Franklin County's 24,000 residents didn't appreciate the national spotlight. Eleven of them, including young Commonwealth's Attorney Charles Carter Lee, signed a petition, in which they called the characterization "preposterous and untrue" and demanded an apology from Prohibition Bureau attorney Frederick C. Dezendorf. However, Dezendorf had bigger problems. Prohibition was still the law of the land, and enforcement was the priority.

But the Democratic Party had Prohibition in its sights. In his Presidential election bid against incumbent Herbert Hoover, Franklin D. Roosevelt made the cause a cornerstone of his campaign. After winning by a landslide, he made good on his promise. A mere 18 days after taking the oath of office, Roosevelt signed into law, on March 22, 1933, the Beer and Wine Revenue Act, modifying the Volstead Act to legalize the sale of beer and wine, and providing for the first time in 13 years a stream of income from alcohol sales that flowed not to criminal syndicates and small-time operators but to the federal government.

The real doozy came next. At 5:32½ p.m. (EST), on December 5, 1933, Utah became the 36th state to ratify the 21st Amendment, repealing the 18th. The nation's dry era was finally and officially over. But it didn't put a stop to moonshining. And that little nugget in the Wickersham report about Franklin County, Virginia? Well, it drew unwanted attention and had serious consequences.

5

MOONSHINE ON TRIAL

The trial was extraordinary. Even some of the big shots—mountain men who had gone into the outlaw liquor business in the new big way—came down out of the hills to testify for the government. The jury was made up pretty much of mountain men from neighboring counties. The mountain men came down, some of them, to convict themselves. They seemed to want it stopped. They seemed to want to go back to the old ways. . . . The big way was too cruel. It brought out too many ugly things in men.

—Sherwood Anderson, "City Gangs Enslave Moonshine Mountaineers," *Liberty*, November 2, 1935

Headlights brightened the two-lane country road out of Callaway, Virginia, as Deputy Sheriff Jeff Richards transported his prisoner to the jail in nearby Rocky Mount. It was 9:30 at night on Saturday, October 12, 1935. From point to point, the trip should have taken no more than 20 minutes. But about halfway into it, near the old Antioch Church of the Brethren, Richards's vehicle was made to stop. By whom, and how, remains unclear, although it is known that the car's emergency brake had been activated. It is also known that Richards's body was found alongside the automobile, at around 11:00 p.m. He'd been brought down by 15 bullets, both buckshot and .45 caliber. The car, a 1931 Ford Model A Roadster, had taken nearly 50 shots—13 in the rear, 12 in the top, and 24 through the windshield. Richards's prisoner, a black man named Jim Smith, who'd been arrested for stealing clothes from a local business, was also dead, having sustained 7 bullet wounds.

News of the ambush startled Franklin County residents, but it was also no surprise. Many in the community believed there could be but one motive for the killings: A federal grand jury was scheduled to convene in just 17 days, and Richards had been expected to testify for his role in an alleged conspiracy ring involving moonshine liquor, tax evasion, and widespread political corruption. He'd already been subpoenaed, and people in town had heard him say that if he were to face time in the penitentiary, he'd take it like a man, but he fully intended to bring others down with him.

Indeed, there were many who had reason to fear for their freedom. Beginning in January 1934, the United States Treasury Department's Alcohol Tax Unit had conducted in rural Virginia a 14-month undercover investigation. The inquiry had been precipitated by the Wickersham Commission report of 1931, which called out Franklin County for its thriving moonshine trade, claiming that 99 out of 100 residents were mixed up in the illicit whiskey business. Citizens and county officials denied the assertion; they even drafted a petition, demanding an official apology. The

Moonshiners were caricatured as backwoods hillbillies. This illustration appeared in *Puck*, December 2, 1903.

feds would do no such thing. Instead, they would use Franklin County as an example, sending a message to illegal distillers and others that moonshining was a serious offense and that evading the tax on spirits would not be tolerated.

Colonel Thomas Bailey, a World War I veteran and award-winning sharpshooter, had been charged with leading the government's work in Franklin County. It was there that he befriended local distillers, learned about their business, ate dinner in their homes, and drank whiskey with them. Purchased it, too.

After seven months on the case, Bailey submitted to his superiors in Washington, D.C., a preliminary report. Dated July 31, 1934, it made clear the gravity of the situation. What was going on in Franklin County went far beyond a bunch of Li'l Abner and Snuffy Smith cartoon hillbilly types firing up their moonshine stills in the hollers. No, what Bailey had uncovered was a political scandal years in the making. He wrote:

> In the fall of 1928, Charles Carter Lee, the Commonwealth's Attorney for Franklin County, Virginia, and Sheriff Pete Hodges called the various deputy sheriffs of Franklin County into the office of Pete Hodges, singly and in pairs, making them a proposition to divide the County up into districts for the purpose of assessing illicit distillers and bootleggers certain amounts (from ten dollars to twenty five dollars) per month for the privilege of operating with the protection of County officers.

Presumably, Jeff Richards was among the county officers summoned by Lee, and his murder must have been fresh in the minds of those filing into the federal courthouse in nearby Harrisonburg when the grand jury met, as planned, on October 29, 1934. In all, more than 200 witnesses would testify. Some feared retribution, and many were reluctant to make known their role in the liquor ring. But testify, they did. Franklin County farmers, gas station owners, store clerks, and delivery men all told of an organization so tightly regulated that few could survive outside of it, forced as they were to purchase raw ingredients from approved sources and to pay protection money to Lee and his associates.

For three months, the grand jury heard witness testimony, and stenographers generated more than 3,000 pages of transcripts.

Finally, on February 7, 1935, the court returned a 22-page blanket indictment, in which 34 individuals and one corporation were charged with conspiring to defraud the United States government of tax revenue from the sale of unlicensed liquor. (An additional 55 people, 3 of whom were dead, including deputy sheriff Richards, were named co-conspirators.) Among the indicted was a former sheriff, a federal investigator, four deputies, a former state prohibition officer named Edgar A. Beckett, and Charles Carter Lee, the same Lee who four years earlier was among those who demanded from Washington, D.C., an apology to Franklin County for singling it out as a locus of illicit distilling.

The following day, federal marshals, accompanied by Colonel Bailey, came to Rocky Mount to issue arrest warrants. One was served upon Lee. But the 29-year-old lawman was not about to be led away in shackles. In a statement, he denied all charges against him. He also refused to resign his post, and remained free on $5,000 bond.

Lee may have appeared confident, but judging by the indictment, it seemed unlikely that things would work out in his favor. Listed in it were 68 "overt acts," 6 of which singled Lee out, accusing him of taking money from illicit distillers, removing a blockade to allow a shipment of illegal liquor to pass through the county, and personally accepting deliveries of five-gallon cans of untaxed spirits. Lee's fellow indictees faced similar charges. The impending trial would be the biggest in the state's history, and the first in a rural area since Prohibition's repeal.

Settled in the late 1700s by Germans and Scots-Irish, Virginia's Blue Ridge Mountain region had an established liquor-making heritage. Nearly every farm had a copper pot still for turning crops into spirits. Apples became brandy. Corn was transformed into whiskey. Producers sold the liquor locally, and to travelers passing through along the Carolina Road, the primary route from Pennsylvania to Carolina backcountry. During the Civil War, whiskey production was banned so as not to divert grain from Confederate troops, who were so desperate for food. When the war was over, farmers once again fired up their stills, but only after being licensed by the federal government, which now laid a tax on liquor.

By 1873, Franklin County was home to 77 distilleries licensed in the state of Virginia. The state went dry some four decades later, in advance of national Prohibition, but the law couldn't stand up to the force of long-standing custom. If people wanted to drink whiskey, there would be others ready to make it. After all, job opportunities in the area remained scarce, and income from liquor sales kept families afloat. And if there was profit to be had by facilitating transactions between buyers and sellers, well, the lure of the dollar was strong. It was no coincidence that Franklin County's liquor trade heated up just as the United States was plunged into the Great Depression.

This was the reality that gave rise to *United States of America vs. Edgar A. Beckett et al.* The "Moonshine Conspiracy Trial," as it came to be known, opened on April 22, 1935, at the United States District Court in Roanoke, Virginia, nearly 200 miles from Rocky Mount, the center of the conspiracy. Seated in the courtroom presided over by Judge John Paul, a bald man with big ears and round dark-framed eyeglasses, were nearly a dozen attorneys representing the accused, all wearing dark three-piece suits and ties, and some 250 spectators, mostly men and a few women of humble means and inquiring minds dressed for court in denim coveralls and flour-sack dresses. Of the 34 people indicted, 4 pleaded guilty, while 7 individuals and the accused corporation, Ferrum Mercantile Company, pleaded no contest. Meanwhile, 23 people entered pleas of not guilty. Among the latter group was Charles Carter Lee.

The next day in court, Lee's attorney, Stephen D. Timberlake, addressed the jury. He offered for his client an unusual defense: "He is a grand-nephew of Robert E. Lee, being a grandson of the elder brother of the South's immortal leader, and he has a name to uphold which would not permit him to stoop to the things that the government charges."

At least one witness would find fault with the familial rationale, including a well-known moonshiner by the name of Thomas Cundiff, who was also charged in the indictment. He was among those who pleaded guilty. He would testify against Lee, explaining that he had given Lee "granny money," or protection fees, of $10 a month, in order to operate his still hassle-free. Refusal to pay the fees, Cundiff explained to jurors, put him at risk of having his still cut up, or destroyed, by members of the liquor ring.

Months earlier, just before the grand jury was seated, Cundiff had been jailed for six weeks in Rocky Mount on an assault charge, then sent to a facility for the criminally insane in Marion, Virginia, where he was held for three months and a day before being released.

HOLLYWOOD MOONSHINE

Moonshining in Franklin County, Virginia, got the Hollywood treatment in the 2012 film *Lawless*. Directed by John Hillcoat, and based on the historical novel *The Wettest County in the World*, by Matt Bondurant, the movie centers on the whiskey-making Bondurant brothers and their often violent exchanges with local law enforcement officers on the take. (Author Bondurant is a descendant of his subjects.) Shia LaBeouf plays the youngest Bondurant. Gary Oldman and Jessica Chastain also star. Film critic A. O. Scott didn't love the film. "This is weak and cloudy moonshine: it doesn't burn or intoxicate," he wrote in his *New York Times* review. Roddy Moore, director of Franklin County's Blue Ridge Institute & Museum, echoed Scott's opinion. "That movie was very entertaining but very incorrect about a lot of things," Moore said. For starters: "It showed them hanging around a still and being drunk. . . . And if you were running a business that had someone who was intoxicated, you would get rid of them." There was simply too much at stake to keep an undisciplined still-hand on the job. Moore's other gripe? The movie was filmed not in Franklin County but at locations in and around Atlanta.

Cundiff told jurors that doctors at Marion could find nothing wrong with him. He blamed his legal troubles on Lee. In response, Lee's attorneys characterized Cundiff as bitter and vengeful.

The trial continued. On Day 7 came testimony from Forrest Bondurant. He told of a violent encounter at Franklin County's Maggodee Creek bridge, on December 19, 1930, where he and his two brothers were kept from crossing by deputy sheriffs Charles Rakes and Henry Abshire, who'd set up a blockade. Bondurant testified that to be allowed passage over the one-lane bridge, the lawmen demanded as payment one of the Bondurants' three vehicles, which were loaded down with 305 gallons of homemade liquor. After some unsuccessful negotiation, Rakes fired at Jack Bondurant, then shot Forrest in the stomach. The confrontation had come after years of kickbacks paid by the Bondurant boys to Abshire to safely operate their stills. During that time, the brothers had sweetened the deal by offering to the lawmen additional payments of whiskey, as well as lumber from their sawmill. Bondurant went on to testify that under this arrangement, Abshire cut the brothers' stills just once, while Deputy Jeff Richards, with whom they did not have such a deal, did so on multiple occasions.

At the start of the third week of trial, May 6, testimony focused on shipments of moonshine-making materials into Franklin County.

SHORT AND SWEET

Franklin County, Virginia, legend tells of a sugar executive who came to the region by train in the 1920s, eager to understand why his company had sold more product in the rural Blue Ridge Mountains than in New York City. All he had to do when he pulled into the railroad depot was look toward the mountains to understand what was going on. Sugar was being turned into liquor, in moonshine stills hidden in the hills. He got on the next train and went right back home.

Based on the quantities, it didn't take much to deduce that the sugar being moved into the county was turning up in something other than pies or biscuits or preserves. Sugar had replaced corn as the main ingredient in moonshine, which was by the 1930s commonly known as "sugar liquor." By studying the books of the Norfolk and Western Railway Company, its chief auditor had determined that between January 1928 and March 1935, an enormous amount of product was making its way into Franklin County. The numbers were astronomical: 1,239,303 pounds of feed, 196,050 pounds of malt, and 65,370 pounds of meal. And the topper: 19,379,633 pounds of sugar, of which 12,863,425 pounds went directly to Ferrum Mercantile Company.

On May 7, testimony shifted to the role of transporters, a position that rated far above "manufacturer" on the moonshining glamour scale. A next-day dispatch from the *Roanoke Times* recapped the latest developments: "Exciting days of the pre-repeal years when whiskey-laden vehicles made a speedway of the Rocky Mount–Roanoke road from the county line into the city were revived in federal district court yesterday. . . ."

Two days after that, jurors heard the testimony of transporter Clarence Mays. He related jaw-dropping tales of caravans 16 cars strong, 14 of them loaded with liquor, and two designated as pilot cars to guide the "trippers," as they were called, along Franklin County's mountainous highways and unpaved back roads. Mays explained how the region's haulers did their business, stopping first at the Blackwater Filling Station to load up their cars with liquor. From there, drivers made their way north to Roanoke, then split up to make deliveries in Lynchburg and Covington, and across the state line in West Virginia. Mays told jurors that on a typical week, he hauled five loads consisting of 100 to 250 gallons of whiskey, estimating that between 1927 and 1933 he had moved out of Franklin County some 130,000 gallons of liquor.

Perhaps one of the most anticipated witnesses to testify at the Moonshine Conspiracy Trial, however, was Willie Carter Sharpe.

She was an ex-con, fresh out of Alderson Federal Prison, in West Virginia. In 1932, she'd begun serving a three-year sentence for violating the National Prohibition Act. A handwritten note on Sharpe's prison ID card says that she'd been "arrested 13 times since 1921 for speeding and reckless driving." In the accompanying photo, Sharpe's wavy, short brown hair, clipped to one side with a barrette, did nothing to temper her menacing scowl and piercing stare. After her appearance before the grand jury in November of 1934, the *Washington Post* noted that her "diamond-studded teeth caused a sensation in the courtroom."

Sharpe's flashy dental work was likely paid for by charging $10 a car, sometimes more, to pilot as many as 10 whiskey-filled automobiles at a time on their runs out of Franklin County. By her own account, Sharpe drove 365 days a year, two to three times a day, and with great skill, racing along steep and winding country roads at speeds of up to 75 miles an hour.

Appearing at the courthouse in Roanoke on May 23 and 24, the government's 165th witness, Sharpe tried to soften her image. Gone was the mouth bling. Wearing white shoes and a hat, and a white dress with ruffled brown sleeves and a collar pinned with a cameo, the 32-year-old Sharpe told the court that between 1927 and 1931,

STILL LIFE

Moonshining in Franklin County isn't just a thing of the past. In 1999, Operation Lightning Strike made public its enduring hold on the region. Federal and state authorities working the case estimated that between 1992 and 1999, local moonshiners produced more than 1.5 million gallons of liquor, defrauding the federal government of $19.6 million in taxes. More recently, a 2013 bust in Penhook, Virginia, uncovered two 800-gallon stills, 1,600 gallons of mash, and nearly 200 gallons of whiskey.

NOV 2, 1935

L*iberty 5¢

HALLOWEEN

TINSEL LADY

A Startling and Revealing
Novel About an American
Star in the Folies-Bergère—
CAN YOU IDENTIFY HER?

by Channing Pollock

CITY GANGS
ENSLAVE
MOONSHINE
MOUNTAINEERS
by Sherwood Anderson

Sherwood Anderson's account of the Franklin County, Virginia, moonshine conspiracy trial reached a national audience in the November 2, 1935, issue of *Liberty* magazine.

she helped move out of the county nearly 145,000 gallons of whiskey. Sharpe, it turned out, had piloted liquor cars for 27 people.

Sharpe also revealed in her testimony that she'd been on a few dates with Jeff Richards, the deputy sheriff who'd been killed just before the grand jury hearing. Once, she said, the two sat together in a parked car as Richards counted out $825 collected from whiskey dealers. He peeled off $25 for Sharpe. When asked in court why Richards gave her the cash, Sharpe was coy. "That's one question I wouldn't like to answer."

Local journalists filed daily reports. Articles about the case also ran in the *Washington Post*, the region's closest big-city paper. Further south, the *Miami Daily News* went for the drama, running a story from the Associated Press that described the "well-paved" road that ran through Franklin County: "Down this mountain highway, taking the torturous curves at top speed, race the cargoes of mountain corn, each loaded car accompanied by a pilot car to block off pursuit."

One writer, however, brought the Moonshine Conspiracy Trial to a national audience. He was Sherwood Anderson, a popular novelist and short story writer of the time, and a mentor to William Faulkner and Ernest Hemingway. The idea to cover the events unfolding in Virginia wasn't Anderson's own. He was asked to go to Roanoke by Treasury Secretary Henry Morgenthau Jr.

What Morgenthau wanted wasn't a play-by-play, but a human-interest piece that would offer readers a glimpse into the lives of rural Americans struggling to make ends meet during the Great Depression. What he wanted was propaganda, but asking Anderson to portray the people of Franklin County not as outlaws but as mountain folk making a living the only way they could was really just asking him to tell the truth about the difficult circumstances in which many people there found themselves. Anderson's story about the trial appeared in the November 2, 1935, issue of the weekly magazine *Liberty*. The headline: CITY GANGS ENSLAVE MOONSHINE MOUNTAINEERS.

Sure, Anderson's language leaned toward exaggeration. The "city" he referred to was Rocky Mount, which hardly registered as a metropolis. And the "gangs"? There was really just one, and it was the one allegedly headed by Charles Carter Lee. Anderson's title was designed to attract eyeballs; his opening paragraph to grab—and keep—readers' attention:

> What is the wettest section in the U.S.A., the place where, during prohibition and since, the most illicit liquor has been made? The extreme wet spot, per number of people, isn't in New York or Chicago. By the undisputed evidence given at a recent trial in the United States Court at Roanoke, Virginia, the spot that fairly dripped illicit liquor, and kept right on dripping it after prohibition ended, is in the mountain country of Southwestern Virginia—in Franklin County, Virginia.

In the piece, Anderson went on to describe Franklin County, to point out the trial's big-name defendant, Charles Carter Lee, and to detail the massive shipments of commodities that didn't make a bit of sense going to a community the size of Rocky Mount. But at the heart of Anderson's story was "the little moonshiner" caught up in a web of illegality spun by unscrupulous "big makers."

Anderson was particularly taken with Willie Carter Sharpe. He wrote of her life as a girl in a small mountain town, and of her employment, while still a child, in a cotton mill, followed by a stint in an overall factory and a five-and-ten store. He told of her marriage to the son of an illegal-liquor tycoon, and of the interviews conducted with her once the trial was over. "It was the excitement got me," she said, explaining to Anderson the lure of leading liquor caravans on high-speed chases as federal officers fired shots at her tires.

Sharpe went on to tell Anderson of high society Virginia women whom she claimed wrote to her after she'd been released from federal prison in hopes that she might take them for a ride. "They wanted to go along with me on a run at night," she said. "They wanted the kick of it." So captivated was Anderson by Sharpe that he went on to write a novel, *Kit Brandon*, in which the title character was loosely modeled after her.

By the time Anderson's *Liberty* article was published, the trial had been over for four months. It ended after 10 weeks, on July 1, 1935. Of the 34 people indicted, 3 were acquitted, including Charles Carter Lee, and 20 were found guilty for their role in the liquor conspiracy that gripped Franklin County for six long years. Eleven pleaded either guilty or no contest. In a statement, Lee said that the charges against him had been "founded in political prejudice" and "anger on the part of criminals whom I prosecuted in their attempt to get vengeance."

Two years passed, and a related trial once again captured the attention of Franklin County residents. The defendants were brothers, Paul and Hubbard Duling, a pair of moonshine runners from West Virginia charged with the murder of Jeff Richards, the deputy sheriff gunned down in 1934. The trial did not last long. It ended in a hung jury. A second one ended in a mistrial. It took three attempts, and a jury drawn from a faraway county, to convict. The men were sentenced to 30 years, far fewer than the 99 recommended by the jury, and sent to the Virginia State Penitentiary.

But in 1948, Paul Duling was paroled, followed a year later by Hubbard. The brothers always maintained their innocence, and in the years that followed their sentencing, two men who had never been tried confessed to killing Richards. Upon their release, the Dulings went back to West Virginia. Whether or not they carried on their whiskey dealing is uncertain. And what of those convicted in the Moonshine Conspiracy Trial a decade earlier? A few, it seems, after serving short sentences, returned to Franklin County and picked up right where they left off.

"DEATH DEFYING DING-DONG DADDIES FROM THE REALM OF SPEED": MOONSHINE AND THE BIRTH OF NASCAR

"Lose on the track, and you go home. Lose with a load of whiskey, and you go to jail."

—Junior Johnson, NASCAR champion
and former moonshine runner

A story passed down over the decades—unconfirmed, yet plausible, given what's known of the man at its heart—tells of an encounter between a highway patrolman and a daring young driver named Lloyd Seay. Seay was a whiskey tripper, well known in North Georgia for his skill behind the wheel and his ability to outrun authorities. His business made him a frequent traveler on the two-lane road between Dawsonville and Atlanta, where he delivered moonshine, sometimes twice a day, racking up more than 150 miles on a round-trip excursion. One day in 1939, Seay was pulled over for speeding. (It must be assumed that he'd unloaded a shipment of moonshine prior to the stop, because if there were whiskey in the car, he definitely would have applied his foot to the gas pedal instead of the brake.) When the officer approached the vehicle, Seay tossed at him two $10 bills.

"Hell, Lloyd, the fine ain't but 10 dollars," the officer supposedly said. To which Seay replied, "I know it, but I ain't gonna have time to stop next time. I'm payin' in advance."

Seay's prowess on the road naturally led to other pursuits. He drove racecars, and performed brilliantly on the track. On November 12, 1938, the 18-year-old took first place in the Armistice Day stock-car race at Atlanta's Lakewood Speedway. Originally planned for 150 miles, the contest was called 15 miles short after a series of accidents left at least two cars wrecked and another in flames. A report in the *Atlanta Constitution* called Seay "the sensation of the race" and told how he came from behind after suffering a pair of flat tires to win the competition in two hours, 29 minutes, 42.8 seconds. Just six months earlier, Seay had been arrested outside a home in Decatur after police searched the vehicle he drove up in and found it packed with 55 gallons of whiskey. Risk taking—whether behind the wheel or with the law—seemed to be part of racing's allure. Sports writers played up the excitement, referring to drivers slated to take part in a New Year's Eve race at Lakewood, on December 31, 1939, as "death defying ding-dong daddies from the realm of speed."

"The Racing Team:" Lloyd Seay, Raymond Parks, and Roy Hall (left to right).

By 1941, Seay was considered "the hottest stock-car driver in the land." On May 31, he drove his '39 Ford coupe to victory at a 50-mile stock-car race at the Allentown fairgrounds, in Pennsylvania. On August 24, he finished first at the 160-mile beach-and-road course in Daytona, Florida, averaging 78 miles per hour, and set a course record. Seay "completely dominated the field," said a newspaper report. A week later, he took first place at a race in High Point, North Carolina. The string of victories made Seay a favorite to win at Lakewood's annual Labor Day extravaganza, where he was scheduled to compete against top drivers, including Bob Flock, Gober Sosebee, and Seay's cousin Roy Hall, all of whom got their start running liquor and staging amateur races in pastures and cornfields to see whose car was faster and which driver the most adept.

At 3:00 p.m. on race day, 23 drivers charged onto the one-mile red-dirt track for the first lap in the 100-mile race. Seay's performance lagged in the beginning. Behind the wheel, with goggles down to keep dust from his eyes, it took Seay 50 turns around the oval before he pulled into first place. By lap 70, Seay appeared to be the driver with the best shot at winning. At lap 80, he was one of 12 men left in the race. Then, with just five miles to go, Seay's engine began to sputter, and to the 15,000 spectators filling the grandstand, flecked with rust-colored dirt, it appeared as if Seay might not cross the finish line. But he pulled through, winning the race in one hour, 29 minutes, and 35.8 seconds. His prize: $450 and a trophy. After taking the championship, the handsome 21-year-old blond grinned as he addressed the crowd. But Seay didn't stick around long. He skipped the evening fireworks display and headed north toward home.

Seay's good fortune would soon change. Early the next morning at his brother Garnett's house near Dawsonville, he was awakened by a knock on the door. His older cousin, Woodrow Anderson, had come to collect $120, the amount he claimed Seay charged

Lloyd Seay's headstone, Dawsonville, Georgia.

to his account at a local market in exchange for sugar. Together, Anderson, Seay, and Garnett ran a whiskey still. Granulated white sugar was added to corn mash to make moonshine. Anderson demanded that the three of them take a drive to visit their Aunt Monnie to have her figure out the numbers and settle the debt. But on the way there, Anderson made two stops, first at his house and then at his father's farm, where he shut off the engine and got out of the car. He approached the back door of the vehicle and suggested to Garnett that he make himself scarce. "I wouldn't get out," Garnett later told police.

With that, Anderson opened the car's back door. Garnett reported that Anderson "jumped on Lloyd and hit him with his fist." From the bib of his overalls Anderson pulled a .32-caliber Smith & Wesson pistol. He shot Garnett in the neck, then turned to Lloyd and fired straight into the young man's heart, killing him instantly.

Race fans must have been shocked when they read the next-day's edition of the *Atlanta Constitution*: "Lloyd Seay, lead-footed mountain boy who didn't care whether he was outrunning revenuers or race-drivers just so long as he was driving fast, was shot to death in a squabble with his cousin yesterday morning. . . ." The article went on to say that law enforcement agents knew Seay "as the most daring of all the daredevil crew" that transported moonshine into Atlanta, and that while they'd often chased after Seay, they rarely caught up with him, as he moved so fast along the treacherous mountain roads that most preferred to simply let him be on his way rather than risk their own lives in pursuit. The article also noted a strange coincidence. Instead of being assigned the usual number 7 for his car in the Labor Day race, Seay's number was switched to the unlucky 13. No explanation was given for the last-minute change.

The case moved quickly through the justice system. On October 31, 1941, Woodrow Anderson was convicted of murder in Lumpkin County Superior Court and sentenced to life in prison. It was later estimated that the cost of the sugar at the center of the dispute that left Seay dead was just $8.75. Sugar at that time cost about five cents a bag, and 175 of those bags would have produced nearly a week's worth of whiskey that would have sold for about $1,500. In those days, the average working person's wage was 40 cents an hour.

Seay was laid to rest at Dawsonville Cemetery, in a grave facing Georgia Highway 9, the "Whiskey Trail" taken by trippers on their way to deliver shine. Chiseled onto the upright tombstone is a bas-relief of Seay's '39 Ford coupe, with a black-and-white photo of Seay fixed under glass in the driver's side window. Etched beneath the car is a trophy to memorialize his final victory. It reads, WINNER, NATIONAL STOCK CAR CHAMPIONSHIP, SEPTEMBER 1, 1941.

Seay's cousin Raymond Parks paid for the monument. A successful businessman, Parks owned the younger man's racing cars. He too had taken to hauling moonshine at an early age. After running away from his parents' home near Dawsonville in 1928, at age 14, Parks supported himself by working as a still hand and moving liquor from Dawsonville to Atlanta and other nearby markets. He did well, and invested his earnings in jukeboxes, vending machines, liquor stores, and fast cars. At the downtown Atlanta garage of mechanic Louis Jerome "Red" Vogt, Parks reunited with Seay and their whiskey-tripping cousin Roy Hall, who'd turned his talent behind the wheel into success at the racetrack. The trio called themselves "the racing team."

Seay's death and America's entry into World War II put the racing team's partnership on pause. Parks went off to Europe to fight in the Battle of the Bulge, and racing events in the States were shut down as part of a wartime effort to save on rubber and gas. In 1945, however, at war's end, racing quickly resumed. One of the first contests was the Labor Day race at Atlanta's Lakewood Speedway, the very event Seay had won four years earlier.

Race fans were thrilled. But not everyone shared their enthusiasm. The *Atlanta Constitution* came out strongly against the race because of a handful of drivers scheduled to compete, noting in an editorial that the men were "some of the more notorious racketeers of the liquor running and bootlegger races." A news item in the same edition reported that 5 of the 15 drivers entered in the race indeed had criminal records. Seay's cousin Roy Hall, of Dawsonville, was among them. Just one month earlier, he'd been sentenced to a year in prison and given a six-month jail term on top of it for taking part in a springtime "bootlegger sweepstakes" along Atlanta's Buford highway. One driver was killed in the contest. Police records showed that since 1937, Hall had been arrested 16 times. Another driver with a rap sheet was Glen "Legs" Law. He'd been on probation since 1942 for an Internal Revenue violation and had recently been indicted for stealing six tons of sugar from an Atlanta bakery. "It will be a shocking display of bad taste if these men are permitted to appear in the race and we respectfully call it to the attention of the proper authorities," the newspaper said.

Another editorial raised further challenges. "These hoodlums, all of them within draft age, have made no contribution to the war. Why were they not in the Army?" it said. "The next question is, where do they get tires good enough to carry on their liquor-car races and liquorrunning?" Throughout the war, Americans had been making do with tires that had been retreaded, hardly the kind of equipment that would be safe for high-speed driving. The writer called on officials to examine drivers' tires before the contest to determine "if they were 'hot,' or illegally obtained."

On race day, 30,000 fans showed up at the venue. Its grandstand was designed to accommodate 5,000, and those without a seat ringed the track instead. Of the five drivers with criminal records, only three showed up, and Lakewood officials promptly banned them from participating. But the decision had an unintended effect. In solidarity, the rest of the drivers refused to race, effectively shutting down the day's entertainment. The 2:30 p.m. start time was delayed, and for almost two hours, city officials and Lakewood owners debated the best way to handle the situation. Meanwhile, the crowd grew restless. They chanted, "We want Hall!"

Fearful that fans might become unruly, officials reversed their earlier decision and kept the original roster intact. At 4:00 p.m., engines roared. "Reckless" Roy Hall won, taking 75 laps around the one-mile track in 74 minutes, and a $600 prize.

In the days and weeks that followed, more than one Labor Day Lakewood racer again found himself on the wrong side of the law. Ed Bagley was arrested twice for speeding the next weekend. The first time, he was racing at 80 miles per hour. The second time, he was zipping along unopposed at nearly the same speed. A week after that, the 27-year-old was found dead of an apparent suicide.

"YOUNG DEMON OF THE HIGHWAYS"

For his audacious road maneuvers and history of "outspeeding the law," Atlanta police described whiskey tripper Roy Hall as "a genius at the wheel." A 1939 article in the *Atlanta Constitution* called Hall a "young demon of the highways," and in 1972, folk singer Jim Croce immortalized the Dawsonville, Georgia, native in "Rapid Roy (The Stock Car Boy)," with lyrics that told of Hall's days running races and nights running shine:

> Oh Rapid Roy, that stock car boy,
> He's the best driver in the land.
> He say that he learned to race a stock car
> By runnin' shine outta Alabam'.
>
> Oh the Demolition Derby and the Figure Eight
> Is easy money in the bank
> Compared to runnin' from the man
> In Oklahoma City with a 500-gallon tank.

Later that month, Roy Hall was sentenced to a one-year prison term after failing to appear at a scheduled court hearing.

A driver named Bill France placed second at the Labor Day race. It was a respectable showing, but France had already begun to shift his attention away from the wheel and onto a new endeavor: the creation of an umbrella organization to oversee stock-car racing. France had driven cars owned by Raymond Parks and raced alongside Lloyd Seay at Lakewood. After Seay's murder, France helped put together a benefit race to collect funds for Seay's elderly parents, who relied on their son's whiskey-hauling income to make ends meet.

Now France focused his energy on forming a governing body for the sport he loved. On December 14, 1947, he convened a group of 35 men, including drivers, mechanics, race promoters, and car owners, in the Ebony Bar at the Streamline Hotel in Daytona Beach, Florida. Atlanta mechanic Red Vogt was there. He'd made his name customizing engines on liquor cars based on the routes taken by their whiskey-tripping drivers. Were the roads bumpy or winding? Vogt made sure that no matter what the conditions, his cars could deliver their cargo unscathed. He suggested a name for the fledgling group: the National Association of Stock Car Auto Racing, or NASCAR.

NASCAR's first race was held February 15, 1948, at a new 2.2-mile oval track designed by France in Daytona Beach. Colorado-born Robert "Red" Byron won the 150-mile competition, in a Ford modified by Vogt and owned by Raymond Parks, the former moonshiner.

Were Lloyd Seay still alive, it's likely he would have gone on to become one of NASCAR's greatest drivers, a speedster sprung from the southern moonshine tradition. But another driver, with a similar background, would go from racing revenue agents to winning accolades on the track. His name was Junior Johnson.

Born June 28, 1931, in Ronda, North Carolina, Robert Glenn

BREAKING RACING'S COLOR BARRIER

Some people call him NASCAR's Jackie Robinson. It's a fitting analogy: Wendell Scott was NASCAR's first African-American driver, breaking the sport's color barrier and becoming the first black driver to win NASCAR's Grand National (now called the Sprint Cup series), on December 1, 1963, at Speedway Park, in Jacksonville, Florida. In 2013, Scott was nominated for induction into the NASCAR Hall of Fame.

Scott was born in Danville, Virginia, on August 29, 1921. As a young man, he found work as a taxicab driver, and later, like so many young men who went on to race cars for a living, as a whiskey tripper, hauling moonshine in a 1940 Ford. In 1952, Scott made his professional NASCAR debut at the Danville Fairgrounds Speedway. Though he faced intense discrimination throughout his career and was often barred from races, Scott went on to compete seven times in the Daytona 500.

In 1977, Scott's story hit the big screen in *Greased Lightning*. The lead role went to comedian Richard Pryor. Pam Grier, of *Foxy Brown* fame, portrayed Scott's wife.

Johnson Jr. came into the world with whiskey in his blood. Distilling was part of the Johnson family DNA. Their Scots-Irish ancestors made whiskey in Pennsylvania in the 1700s. Eventually, the Johnson forebears made their way south along the Appalachian Trail, settling in the foothills of North Carolina's Blue Ridge Mountains. It was there that Johnson's father carried on the legacy. At one point, so much whiskey was stored in the family home that young Junior and his siblings—L.P., Fred, Ruth, and Annie Mae (Shirley wasn't born yet)—had to scale boxes to climb into bed at night.

In 1935, revenue agents raided the Johnson home, removing from it more than 7,200 gallons of clear corn whiskey. It took all day to cart the booze out of the house. To speed the work, agents set

WANTED

information from **YOU** the taxpayer on the locations of

BOOTLEG STILLS

Moonshine stills in your locality like that pictured above, are robbing you of many thousands of dollars in Federal and State liquor taxes. Help your Government by reporting them, by mail or phone, to

ALCOHOL AND TOBACCO TAX DIVISION, INTERNAL REVENUE SERVICE

Alcohol and Tobacco Tax
Post Office Box 224
Bluefield, West Virginia   Phone 9312

**All communications held
strictly confidential**

Form 1793 (5-54)

U. S. TREASURY DEPARTMENT, INTERNAL REVENUE SERVICE

16—70765-1   GPO

U.S. Treasury Department poster, circa 1949.

boards on the stairs of the two-story dwelling and slid the packages down one by one. To four-year-old Junior and his oldest brother, L.P., the makeshift slides looked fun. They hopped on the liquor boxes and rode them from the second floor to the first. The agents didn't like that, and they let the children know. But L.P. was sassy, telling the agents that it was his home and that the brothers would do as they pleased.

Meanwhile, the men continued their work, arranging cases and cans and jars of whiskey on the family's front lawn. A photograph taken at the time shows boxes stacked five high, nearly up to a man's neck, in at least 20 rows, several boxes deep, just beyond the home's neatly trimmed hedges. What came next isn't pictured: Officers smashed the containers, allowing all that good whiskey to seep into the soil. The bust sent Johnson's father to prison on a five-year sentence.

By 14, Johnson had dropped out of the eighth grade, and he turned to transporting moonshine for his dad. His runs were local, at first. But by the time Johnson was 16, he was venturing further from home, hauling whiskey "all night long, every night" to bootleggers in Lexington, Greensboro, Salisbury, and Albemarle, among other places, some 50 to 100 miles away. The way he saw it, delivering moonshine was the same as delivering milk.

His car was a 1940 Ford, modified to the hilt, with fat tires for stability, extra big rims, and springs to help handle the weight of the liquor. "It was a good drivin' car," Johnson recalls. "Very durable." By removing the seats from the passenger side and back, he could fit inside the vehicle 22 cases of moonshine, 12 half-gallon jars to the box. He sold the liquor for about $10 a gallon and pocketed two of those dollars for himself. The cargo he stacked to just below the windows, so passing motorists couldn't see what he was carrying.

Beyond storage capacity, however, it was a car's engine that mattered most to a whiskey tripper. The Ford's V-8 engine was fast, sure, but to make that car fly it needed a transplant. Ambulances had the best engines—Cadillac engines, supercharged. "It was an overhead valve engine," Johnson says. "Nobody had ever seen anything like it." The only way for a driver to get his hands on one of those engines was if an ambulance crashed, or somehow or other ended up in the junkyard or for sale by the city. Johnson paid attention. He had to have those engines. "They were faster to start with, and when you souped them up they were tremendous," he says. "They were faster than anything that the revenuers had."

Speed was critical if you wanted to keep from getting caught. But a driver also needed courage and quick reflexes. On the roads that ran out of Wilkes County, Johnson perfected his moves. One came to be called the "bootleg turn," and it involved slowing the car down, dropping the gear into second, punching the brake, and spinning the car around in the opposite direction of those who were giving chase. To fool agents, Johnson had lights and a siren that he'd place on his vehicle when he needed to get his liquor through a blockade. His tactics worked every time. Not once was Johnson nabbed while hauling whiskey.

Other drivers weren't so lucky. But in rural North Carolina, opportunities to make money on the right side of the law were few, and making, selling, and moving moonshine guaranteed an income, so people took their chances. Few people looked down on the business. In fact, Wilkes County was so full of whiskey trippers that in 1947, the local racetrack invited them to come on out and drive in the hour and a half that passed between qualifying races and the main show.

"I was 16, barefooted, plowing a mule, planting corn for my father," Johnson told *Sports Illustrated*'s Ed Hinton about his first race. His brother, L.P., came to Johnson in the field and told him what was going on at North Wilkesboro Speedway. "He wanted me to drive his liquor car, a '40 Ford, in the race." It was an interesting request since L.P. and Junior's other brother, Fred, were also hauling liquor and were experienced drivers. Says Johnson, "L.P. figured I had a little more nerve." His brother was right. Johnson placed second.

"That's the first time I raced anything or raced anybody," Johnson

HERO WORSHIP

Released in 1973, *The Last American Hero* stars Jeff Bridges as Junior Jackson, a character modeled after NASCAR superstar Junior Johnson. The film is based on Tom Wolfe's 1965 *Esquire* article "The Last American Hero Is Junior Johnson. Yes!" Although the movie's timeline doesn't exactly follow Johnson's personal timeline—it portrays the fictional Jackson's rise as a stock car driver in the early '70s, while Johnson got his start in the '50s and retired in 1966—its arc is true to Johnson's biography as a farm boy fascinated by fast cars, who enters the world of professional racing while his father, a moonshiner, serves time in prison.

recalls. "I had been outrunnin' revenuers for a long time. And when they run that race, it kinda stuck with me that that would be a good future for me, and as time went along, I just got deeper and deeper and deeper."

Johnson made his NASCAR debut on September 7, 1953, at Darlington Raceway, in South Carolina. He crashed. His first NASCAR win was at Hickory Motor Speedway, in North Carolina, in 1955. That year, Johnson placed first in five races.

His July 29 win at the Altamont-Schenectady Fairgrounds, in New York, however, would be the last of the run. After racing his '55 Oldsmobile to victory and taking the $900 prize in the 100-mile contest, Johnson got back behind the wheel and drove south all night to North Carolina, pulling up to the family home at around 4:00 a.m. What happened next would put his racing career on hold.

"My dad had a still back in the woods, and they fire 'em up before daylight so nobody can see the smoke," Johnson recalls. "He was gonna run his mash and make his whiskey that day, and when I come in, he'd overslept. He asked me if I'd go in and fire his stills so the smoke would be gone when he got there."

Johnson did what was asked of him. But just as he was about

NASCAR legend and former moonshine runner Junior Johnson, in 1985.

to put coke on the flame, he found that the place had been staked out. Eighteen revenue agents were waiting for him out there in the woods, he says. Johnson threw the coke in one agent's face and took off on foot. But his chance of escaping was slim. "He told me there wasn't no use running," Johnson remembers. Charged with "manufacturing non-tax-paid whiskey," he was sentenced to two years at the federal prison in Chillicothe, Ohio. He served 11 months and three days.

Johnson returned to racing when he got out. But doing time had left him bitter. "I had kind of a chip on my shoulder," Johnson says. Instead of getting out of the whiskey game and focusing solely on his racing career, he kept right on moonshining, using his earnings from the track to supply raw materials and financial support to partners who worked the backwoods stills. "I just went back into it. Got bigger and bigger in it," he says. But things changed in 1960. "They was after me so hot I just had to quit. I quit and I just went on to racing. I just let it go," Johnson says. That year, Johnson won the Daytona 500.

It wasn't long before writer Tom Wolfe profiled Johnson in the March 1965 issue of *Esquire* magazine. "The Last American Hero Is Junior Johnson. Yes!" solidified the legend of the whiskey tripper transformed into a NASCAR superstar, with Wolfe characterizing Johnson as a "good old boy" who *really* made good.

Johnson retired from racing the following year. He was 35 years old, and in his 14 years with NASCAR, he'd won 50 out of 310 races. But for Johnson, racing on a track never held the same allure as racing revenuers on the open road. "I just got aggravated with it," he told Ed Hinton, of *Sports Illustrated.* "I'd go to a dern race somewhere and I'd done won it two or three times, and it wasn't any fun. You're just going back over and over." He transitioned into team ownership. When Johnson left motorsports in 1995, he'd helped 38 drivers take first place in 139 races.

President Ronald Reagan pardoned Johnson for his

moonshining conviction, in 1986, the day after Christmas. In 1998, *Sports Illustrated* named Johnson the greatest driver that ever lived. Today, he makes his home in Charlotte, North Carolina, about 90 minutes south of the one he grew up in and the site of the track where he ran his first race. He's honored in both the National Motorsports Press Association and North Carolina Sports Halls of Fame. In 2010, Johnson was inducted into the Inaugural Class of the NASCAR Hall of Fame.

Among NASCAR's Hall of Fame nominees for 2013 was Raymond Parks, who as a young man invested the money he made from moonshining into a career as a racing team owner, paying for the cars driven by Lloyd Seay and Roy Hall, and providing early financial support for Bill France's newborn NASCAR. Parks died in 2010 at the age of 96. When Hall of Fame voting closed, however, he was not among the five candidates to make the final cut.

Junior Johnson, for one, always thought Parks had long ago earned his place among NASCAR greats. "He contributed money and stuff to help 'em get it off the ground," Johnson said of Parks in an Espn.com interview. "I'd have to give him credit for being the first contributor to the sport. . . . He backed it, plumb up to the day his end came." He continued, "I just think he's one of the greatest people I ever met in the sport."

"POPSKULL CRACKDOWN"

"Remember . . . Moonshining
is a National Disgrace!"

—From the U.S. government-issued comic book
"Don't be a 'Sugar Daddy' to Moonshiners!," 1957

Moonshiners and revenuers. For children of a certain era, in certain parts of the country, this was a popular game, like cops and robbers, or cowboys and Indians. It was all about the chase, of good guys going after the bad. It was a game rooted in popular culture, based on nearly a century of law enforcement efforts by the U.S. Treasury Department, which in 1957 described the government's ongoing work in the fight against illicit alcohol as "a persistent search for and seizure of individual stills and operators."

Indeed, a report issued in 1955 by the trade association Licensed Beverage Industries Inc. (LBI) noted that in the previous year, federal, state, and local agents had captured an "unprecedented" 22,913 stills capable of producing each year about 36 million gallons of non-tax-paid liquor. Annual output was probably double that, given the fact that there most certainly were thousands more stills that went undetected, which meant that by midcentury, more than a quarter of all distilled spirits made and sold in the United States were of the illicit variety. "The moonshine problem is huge. It is dangerous. It is spreading," the report warned.

The feds didn't need LBI to tell them about the moonshine menace. After the lifting of World War II restrictions on sugar and copper, which was used to make whiskey stills, the moonshine business boomed. Something had to be done to stop it, and by 1957, the Internal Revenue Service (formerly the Bureau of the Internal Revenue) had taken its moonshiners-and-revenuers game to a level previously unseen, switching up their strategy in the fight against illicit distilling by instituting a three-point plan. First, concentrate on finding and prosecuting networks of big-time operators. Second, extend investigations—watch and wait—until more violators could be rounded up at once. And third, crack down on the sale of raw materials needed to produce and package moonshine whiskey. The *Wall Street*

Journal called the government's enhanced anti-moonshine push a "popskull crackdown."

It was the third part of the plan—the Preventive Raw Materials Program—that was perhaps most visible to the general public. Posters printed and distributed by the United States Treasury Department's Alcohol Tax Unit (ATU) began appearing outside general stores and supermarkets throughout the Southeast, part of an aggressive campaign to cut off the supply of ingredients used to make illegal liquor.

> WE DON'T SELL SUGAR TO MOONSHINERS
> 100 pounds makes enough moonshine to
> defraud our government of $105.00 in taxes.
> WE WILL NOT BE THE MOONSHINER'S PARTNER IN CRIME

A sign on the front door, however, didn't stop back-door transactions, and plenty of merchants and moonshiners went about their business as usual. To sugar refineries, wholesalers, and retailers, the ATU also distributed a 12-page educational comic book designed to shed light on the problem and enlist supporters in the fight to stamp out illicit liquor production. Its title: *Don't Be a "Sugar Daddy" to Moonshiners!* The cover showed a scowling sack of sugar in a top hat and tux. Inside, a man hunches over a plate scooping whole packs of sugar into his fang-filled mouth: "BOOTLEG BOSSES Must have sugar to exist!"

Despite the fact that most moonshining was taking place in the Southeast, the ATU's efforts weren't confined to the region. Moonshining was a problem in Detroit, New York City, and Philadelphia. In Chicago, Treasury Department agents, or T-men, met with representatives from some of the country's largest sugar refineries and industrial consumers to get big hitters on their team, figuring that moonshiners cut off by local vendors would eventually reach out to them to replenish their supply. Either

Detail, "Don't Be a 'Sugar Daddy' to Moonshiners!" This 1957 IRS comic book warned sugar suppliers about the sinister intentions of some of their customers.

that, or they'd switch from buying sugar in 100-pound bags to purchasing scores of 2-pound boxes. Voluntary monitoring was the goal, but in lieu of it, the feds intended to force compliance, requiring companies to report on a daily basis all of the sugar coming in and out of their facilities.

The government's watch list extended to other items as well. As part of the raw materials program, the feds kept close tabs on fruit jars, tin cans, glass jugs, and other supplies associated with illegal liquor production. According to a 1961 article that appeared in the *Hartford Courant*, a "container pinch" would lead some moonshiners to package their product in plastic squeeze bottles as well as "plastic bags encased in corrugated paper boxes, gasoline and paint cans, and bottles retrieved from public trash dumps."

Enforcement efforts seemed to be paying off. But the government's fight against moonshiners didn't let up. Economics was one reason for moonshine's persistence. In the mid 1950s, it took about 10 pounds of sugar, worth $1, to make a gallon of moonshine. The wholesale cost on a gallon of white whiskey varied depending on where it was sold, but in Georgia, prices ran between $14 and $18. Diluted moonshine could then be purchased from bootleggers by the pint and in pool halls, gas stations, and roadside shacks by the drink. Price-wise, moonshine was a good deal for consumers. With the federal tax on distilled spirits at $10.50 a proof gallon (a gallon of spirits that is 50% alcohol), up from $2 in the years immediately following Prohibition, many people couldn't afford legal booze. Where a pint of moonshine might run between $1.75 and $2.50, the same quantity of the least-expensive legal whiskey sold for about $2.80. LBI was none too happy to be competing for business with tax cheats, and they made a point of studying the problem and advocating for lower tax rates on distilled spirits. After more than six decades, however, federal tax rates remain the same.

AMERICAN MOONSHINE ABROAD

In the 1950s, Americans in Saudi Arabia employed by U.S. oil companies were at one point given permission by the Saudis to import alcohol for personal use. But this changed when locals working with the Americans developed a liking for the "devil's water." Their liquor supply cut off, some Americans turned to homemade hooch. One woman, in Saudi Arabia with her husband, shared her recipe:

> Get a five-gallon juice jug. Put in 10 pounds of sugar; five cans of concentrated orange juice; add some grain yeast; fill up the jug with water; add raisins and dried apples, and let it ferment in a warm place for about two weeks.

Distilling the blend, she said, resulted in some of the best homemade hooch "south of Beirut and east of Suez."

Two decades later, American diplomats in Libya were also coming up with their own methods for turning everyday ingredients into potent liquors. One woman made "white lightning" or "flash" from pulverized and fermented potatoes and raisins.

Just as they did during Prohibition, many clandestine distillers continued to pump out bad booze, employing unscrupulous production methods that prioritized quantity and speed over flavor and purity. One writer would later say white lightning "tastes like a mixture of cheap Scotch and bad beer and smells like a beer-soaked undershirt after a party." In 1958, just one year after the government stepped up its enforcement efforts, 27 people in New York died from a batch of poisoned liquor. Around that same time, tainted alcohol was also implicated as the cause of death in Chattanooga, Tennessee; Philadelphia; and Revere, Massachusetts.

Moonshiners, it seemed, weren't the least bit remorseful. One man responded incredulously when asked by federal agents why he didn't drink his own handcrafted liquor. "Man, do you think I'm crazy?" he said. "I don't want to kill myself. I like whisky lots better than wine, but I'd rather drink wine than drink that stuff I been making in that steel drum."

The hazards were numerous. Some illicit distillers dosed their mash with Red Devil lye, a drain opener, to speed fermentation. Others built stills out of scrap metal soldered at the seams with lead, and turned old car radiators into condensers to cool the alcohol vapors and convert them into liquid. Lead salts leached from the condenser were shown to cause, if not death, then convulsions and delirium followed by coma.

To address growing safety concerns, the federal government in 1960 rolled out its Poison Moonshine Publicity Program. Included in the effort was a series of public service announcements aimed at southern audiences. Paul Coates, a prominent newspaper columnist at the time, noted the jarring effect of hearing on country-music radio the sonorous voice of *Double Indemnity* actor Edward G. Robinson:

> Ladies and gentlemen, did you know there's a killer loose in your community? Moonshine whisky. Deadly poisons have been found in 91% of the moonshine confiscated in the South. The moonshiner is a racketeer with an organization and a plan for your destruction. The victims of these racketeers never complain. Dead men can't talk. Don't drink moonshine. It will kill you.

Louis Armstrong recorded a different announcement for black audiences:

WARNING

DEADLY POISON
Moonshine Liquor
Being Distributed Locally

DO NOT DRINK ANY Type of BOOTLEG LIQUOR regardless of source. **DEADLY POISONOUS** Lead Salts are being found in WHITE LIQUOR. This poison can cause **DEATH** or serious illness as much as a year after drinking.

The next SMALL DRINK May Bring the amount of Lead Salts in the Body to the concentration point necessary to cause **DEATH!**

DR. J. W. R. NORTON
State Health Director

This 1960s-era poster was part of a North Carolina public health campaign.

Fans like this were produced by the IRS and distributed throughout the South. This one is from Alabama, circa 1960.

DEADLY POISON

Moonshine

Being Distributed Locally!

You Can Help Stamp Out Moonshine . . .

Report Violations To The Federal Alcohol, Tobacco and Firearms Division

Anniston 237-2121	Jasper 348-6696
Birmingham . . 325-3244	Mobile 433-3581
Decatur. 355-7170	Ext. 216
Dothan 792-1577	Montgomery . . 263-7521
Florence 764-4641	Ext. 452
Gadsden 547-7241	Opelika 745-5372
Haleyville. . . . 486-3413	Selma 872-1693
Huntsville . . . 536-8012	Sylacauga . . . 245-4153
Jackson 246-4878	Tuscaloosa. . . 758-7739

INTERNAL REVENUE SERVICE

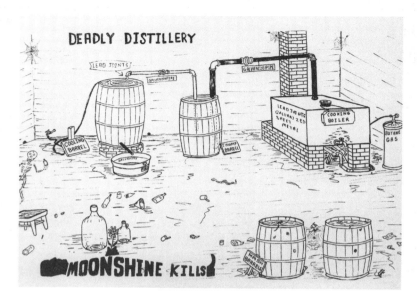

As part of its anti-moonshine campaign the U.S. government offered this illustrated look at the unsanitary conditions inside a clandestine distillery, circa 1960.

Hey, gang, Old Satchmo here, with a message for my good friends. Did you know that poison moonshine is killing folks in your community? You don't have to be one of those suckers. That junk will blind, paralyze, and eventually kill you, friends. When old Satchmo blows out your favorite blues, I'd sure like for you to be around to listen. So take care of yourself. Don't drink pure poison. It'll kill you, hear?

State health departments also did their part to educate people about the potentially lethal effect of illegal whiskey. In the Carolinas, billboards and posters appeared emblazoned with huge skulls and crossbones to alert people to its danger. Bumper stickers were distributed, too.

What one North Carolina poster explained that the celebrity announcers did not was that moonshine's effect was often cumulative. "DEADLY POISONOUS Lead Salts are being found in WHITE LIQUOR," the poster said. "This poison can cause DEATH or serious illness as much as a year after drinking." Tests backed up the claim. Steady drinkers were shown to face serious health consequences as lead salts built up in their bodies.

What more could be done? In 1962, the federal government launched Operation Dry-Up, an experimental program to combat the illicit whiskey trade in one southern state. The goal was to put "unremitting pressure on the violator by an enlarged investigative force." The feds hailed the program as an unqualified success, noting that the unnamed state in which Operation Dry-Up was based had seen the "almost complete elimination of the commercial violator." Further, the feds estimated a concomitant rise in tax revenue from the sale of legal liquor within the state to the tune of $2.4 million. In hopes of replicating the results of Operation Dry-Up, the program was expanded to a second state in 1966, and a third in 1968.

By the 1970s, the making and drinking of moonshine appeared to be in decline. Several factors contributed to the change. One, improved techniques employed by federal agents to track down stills, including aerial photography and the use of a heat-seeking device able to pinpoint from an aircraft distilleries hidden in the woods, had pushed not a few long-time makers to close up shop rather than risk getting caught. Another factor: Fewer dry counties in which bootlegging could flourish. What's more, Mississippi in 1969 became the last to end statewide prohibition, 36 years after national Prohibition came to a close. Finally, there was money. While lack of it led to moonshine's rise, higher incomes and greater job opportunity meant more people were able to afford legal liquor.

"People get a little money in their pocket and they get sort of fancy, want to get away from jugs into the bottled in bond stuff," one North Carolina moonshiner told a newspaper reporter. He was referring to whiskey bottled and stored in accordance with regulations established by the federal government. Drinking it conferred status; moonshine was low-class.

But there was another factor at play in moonshine's decline: inflation. By 1974, the cost of sugar had risen exponentially, to more than $40 per 100-pound sack, more than a tripling of price in the space of a year. At the time, a gallon of moonshine was selling for between $8 and $12. Why pay a higher price and risk the health consequences when you could buy a $2 pint of legal bourbon? The math, and the risk, just didn't make sense.

Tastes were changing, too. By the 1970s, marijuana had become an important cash crop throughout the South. On still-hunting expeditions through moonshine country, investigators often found tall green cannabis plants hidden alongside rows of corn. Then, as if to drive home the point that the moonshine business had taken a hit with pot's rise, a pair of North Georgia "moonshine czars," Garland "Bud" Cochran and Ben Kade "Junior" Tatum, were indicted in a South Carolina federal court in the summer of 1974 for arranging an airlift of marijuana from Colombia to the U.S. on a DC-4 jet. A decade earlier, the ATF noted, Cochran had been shipping into Atlanta 7,000 gallons of moonshine a month.

There remained plenty of moonshiners, however, who disavowed the shift to weed. "Some of the old-timers wouldn't raise it. They think it's awful. It's against their code of ethics. It's these new people who're into marijuana," one federal agent explained in a 1977 article in the *Washington Post*. It was easy to understand. Marijuana simply didn't fit into traditional mountain culture. Making moonshine was folk art. Growing marijuana was not.

Still, moonshining was perceived by many to be an art that was dying. By 1978, federal agents had seized just 361 moonshine stills. The number was remarkably low. In 1935, two years after the end of Prohibition, agents seized 15,712 stills, and in 1965, the number of seizures stood at 7,432. Whiskey production was down. So was enforcement of federal liquor laws.

Revenue agents never gave up completely on the fight against illicit alcohol. As long as there were people making it, keeping money from government coffers, the law would be on it. One of the more unusual raids took place in Franklin County, Virginia, in 1979. The still site was underground. Moonshiners had used a bulldozer to dig out a room-size pit that they then concealed with a roof made of sod. Aboveground they placed cinderblocks painted to look like headstones, at which they placed flowers. They mowed the lawn regularly and kept the grounds looking neat. Underneath were eighteen 800-hundred gallon stills. Having exposed the so-called cemetery still, agents posed for a picture in the pit before using explosives to destroy the operation.

With moonshiners coming up with ever more creative ways to conceal their stills, federal agents, in turn, had to devise equally crafty ways of catching offenders at work. One master of the game was C. Garland Bunting. A revenue agent in Halifax County, North Carolina, since 1953, Bunting nabbed lawbreakers by blending in and "talkin' trash." He explained his technique in a 1982 *Wall Street Journal* article:

> When you back in these ol' hick places, you got to be a hick. . . . If a man hunts coons, then I hunt coons. If he's selling antiques, I'm buying antiques. If he's a farmer, I'm a farmer.

In one undercover effort, Bunting posed as a fish peddler driving a beat-up pickup truck. He drew crowds by playing harmonica and singing funny songs: "String out your dishpan, here comes the fishman." No one suspected the eccentric fishmonger of being a snitch, which made it easy for Bunting to get a moonshiner to sell him booze, then turn around and set the man up for busting.

Today, moonshine busts tend to uncover marijuana and methamphetamines, maybe even firearms. Others reveal a region's deep-seated folkways and a community's displeasure with law enforcement officers whom they feel would better serve the people by concentrating their efforts on bigger problems. A moonshine bust in Cocke County, Tennessee, in 2013, provided a perfect example of the latter.

"This is the way our county lives," a neighbor said when interviewed by a local television news reporter. "This is all this boy knows." The boy to whom the woman was referring was a grown man alleged to have at his home-based plant between 15 and 18 moonshine stills. According to a worker, the stills were fired up each morning at 5:00 a.m. and ran until noon, producing by the end of the day 15 cases of white liquor. Locals say the man's family had been making moonshine since the 1960s. A quart of the legal stuff sells in Gatlinburg, Tennessee, for $35, the neighbor noted. But you can get your hands on a quart of quality product in Cocke County, she said, for $10 to $12.

It's a good deal for the consumer, and good for the maker, too, since his profit isn't dented by the payment of taxes. Yet each bottle of shine represents significant risk. Penalties for illicit distilling are steep. At the federal level, a person found guilty of making and selling moonshine faces up to 10 years in prison, a $10,000 fine, or both.

But increasingly, state liquor laws have been relaxed, paving the way for legitimate businesses to revive the art of making raw, unaged corn whiskey. Most do it the old-fashioned way, without a single teaspoon of sugar in the recipe.

MOONSHINE RENAISSANCE

"Well, between Scotch and nothin', I suppose I'd take Scotch. It's the nearest thing to good moonshine I can find."

—William Faulkner

As a teenager growing up in Harlan County, Kentucky, in the 1990s, Colin Spoelman didn't have much experience with moonshiners. But he was familiar with local bootleggers, including a silver-haired woman named Maggie Bailey. Harlan County was dry, and Bailey, who was known as Mag, was a well-known source for booze. She ran the business out of her home, selling brands like Bud Ice, Boone's Farm, and Zima, all of it at a markup. The work kept her young, she said. By all accounts, Bailey started bootlegging in 1920, at age 16. By the time Spoelman was 16, Bailey was in her ninth decade.

For college, Spoelman headed north, to Yale. After graduating, he settled into a second-floor walkup apartment in Williamsburg, Brooklyn, a neighborhood that had already developed a reputation as a kind of hipster paradise. His taste in liquor, and perhaps for adventure, too, had evolved, and on trips home to Harlan County, Spoelman would pick up jugs of moonshine and bring them back to Brooklyn, where the liquor was a novelty with his friends. Wary, they'd take one or two sips, at most. The year was 2005. "Moonshine was sort of at a low point for its sex appeal," Spoelman says. "People really thought that it would kill them."

Eventually, though, Spoelman's moonshine supply ran low, and he decided to have a go at making his own whiskey. For $700, from a website called Brewhaus.com, he and his friend, David Haskell, purchased a small eight-gallon still, hot plates, and fermenters, in which to steep grain. He read distilling how-to books, did a few trial runs, and only once had a mishap, the result of making mash incorrectly and burning it at the bottom of the still. "That superheated the hot plate and it melted the kitchen countertop," says Spoelman. "That was the only permanent damage that was ever done, to my knowledge."

Before long, Spoelman had produced a batch of white whiskey far smoother than the "volatile, high-proof" spirit he was used to. And unlike much of the moonshine coming out of Appalachia,

Spoelman's was made from corn. ("No sugar," he says of his recipe. "That was always a point of pride.") His urban moonshine was popular, and he began to sell it from his apartment. But as Spoelman notes, his customers didn't have a reference point for comparison. "Aside from Georgia Moon and a couple commercial brands, there really wasn't anything out there for people to know what unaged whiskey tastes like," he says. "And yet there were also people who were becoming more and more interested in whiskey."

Spoelman was inspired. He began researching how to turn his extralegal hobby into a legitimate business. Home distilling, unlike home brewing and winemaking for personal use, was then and continues to be illegal in the United States. But as it turned out, a new law aimed at supporting agriculture in New York State made it easier and less expensive to start a small-batch distillery. And so it was that in 2010, Spoelman and Haskell opened Kings County Distillery, the first legal distillery in New York City since Prohibition ended in 1933. The pair's inaugural spirit was an unaged corn whiskey. Moonshine. Sold in glass bottles shaped like a pocket flask. "They've proved to be popular because of their portability," Spoelman says.

Moonshine, of course, is a misnomer for any spirit sold legally in the United States. The government's Alcohol and Tobacco Tax and Trade Bureau, commonly known as the TTB, does not recognize moonshine as an official class or type of distilled spirit. But *moonshine* has resonance. Some consumers respond to the word positively, associating it with American history and tradition, with danger and excitement, or, as in Spoelman's case, *home*. For others, the name is totally off-putting, and they assume that a product called moonshine will taste of nail polish and turpentine and cause a drinker to go blind. Look closely at a label to see a spirit's true designation. Most "moonshines" are officially categorized as either *corn whisky* (spelled by the government without the *e*), or *grain neutral spirits*, which are in the same class as vodka. Historically,

Junior Johnson's Midnight Moon is America's best-selling moonshine.

much of the moonshine made in Appalachia was either a mixture of corn and sugar, or entirely sugar based.

Junior Johnson's Midnight Moon, made by Piedmont Distillers, in Madison, North Carolina, is the country's best-selling moonshine. It's named for the moonshine runner turned NASCAR driver. In 2012, Piedmont sold 120,000 cases of Midnight Moon, according to food and beverage industry analyst Technomic. The whiskey is available online and through distributors, and in all 50 states at mainstream retailers such as Walmart, Walgreens, Publix, Safeway, and big-box store Costco. "That's a mind-bender," Piedmont founder Joe Michalek says of the last one on the list.

Midnight Moon comes in several flavors, including cherry, strawberry, cranberry, blackberry, and blueberry, all spiked with pieces of real fruit; the Apple Pie flavor is made with apple juice and cinnamon stick, a formulation that's long been enjoyed by moonshine drinkers.

The line's top seller, however, is the Original, made from a corn mash redistilled three times and bottled at 80 proof, or 40% alcohol by volume. The recipe is based on one used by Junior Johnson's father, who made white liquor in the Carolina hills. "Any more authentic and it would be illegal," says the brand's website, a virtual homage to the Johnson legend. On prominent display is the 1956 mug shot from Junior Johnson's one and only moonshining arrest, the one that sent him to the federal pen for nearly a year.

Midnight Moon Original would come more than 50 years after that arrest. But it didn't come easy. When Michalek opened his distillery in 2005, he started with a spiced moonshine called Catdaddy. For his next product, Michalek, a New York native, dreamed of making moonshine with his adopted state's most famous former moonshiner, Junior Johnson. Michalek was acquainted with Johnson through NASCAR Winston Cup racing. Johnson, a big man with a thick head of silver hair, was a team owner, and Michalek had once worked for race sponsor R.J. Reynolds Tobacco. One day, he and Junior had breakfast at a local restaurant called Duke's, and Michalek did his best to sell the idea. It didn't take.

A year passed. Michalek was addressing a group of Rotary Club members. His cell phone rang. He could see from the display that it was the distillery calling. He was in the middle of his talk, however, so he didn't pick up. They "called and called," Michalek says. When he called back he got the message he'd been waiting for: *Junior Johnson wants to visit the distillery.* By 11:00 the next morning, Johnson and a friend were touring the facility, located in an old train depot. "He asked what's all involved," Michalek says of Johnson. He wanted to know what it took to be legit.

Michalek developed prototypes, trying to perfect the flavor of Johnson family moonshine. He brought samples to Johnson and a group of Johnson's friends gathered for breakfast at the older man's garage. When Michalek showed up, the place was filled with the sweet, heady scent of country sausage, pork fatback, and caramelized apples. Bacon and split hotdogs sizzled on the grill. Biscuits, grits, sliced tomato, and scrambled eggs rounded out the offerings. This roomful of good old boys was game to give Michalek's clear whiskey a try. In true Appalachian style, they passed around a jar, each man taking a sip. Somebody mixed a bit of it with Coke. And as Michalek tells it, the response went something like this: "Damn, Junior. We've been trying to make liquor this good for 50 years." With that, Johnson, dressed in overalls, gave his approval. "Okie dokie," he said.

Today, Johnson is a partner in Piedmont Distillers. In a television interview with *North Carolina Now*, he related his satisfaction with the business and with the product that bears his name. "Being in that environment and working with the people that did the moonshine like it's supposed to be, you're very proud of it. You don't have one batch good and one batch bad or something of that nature. They duplicate it exactly like it's supposed to be every time."

Does Johnson have a favorite flavor? "I'm not a big drinker," he says. "You can't drink whiskey and drive them fast cars."

Coming in a strong second in moonshine sales is Ole Smoky Tennessee Moonshine, in Gatlinburg, Tennessee. Of all the bottles of corn whiskey sold in the U.S. in 2012, 100,000 of them were filled with Ole Smoky. At 12 750-milliliter jars to a case, that's 1.2 million jars total. Company founder Joe Baker is a criminal lawyer by trade, and an East Tennessee native. He jumped at the chance to open a distillery when, in 2009, state legislators eager to create economic opportunities for farmers and small business owners passed a bill that made it legal for distilleries to operate statewide instead of in select counties only. Opened in 2010, Ole Smoky is Tennessee's first legal moonshine distillery.

Like Midnight Moon, Ole Smoky moonshine is sold in Mason jars and is available at retailers across the country. The liquor comes in four main varieties: Original ("for sippin'"), White Lightnin' ("for mixin'"), Moonshine Cherries ("A party in a jar!"), and Apple Pie ("Americana in a jar"). The latter was in 2013 named Best of Class in the American Distilling Institute's Artisan American Spirits competition.

The flagship distillery, in downtown Gatlinburg, is perhaps one of the most entertaining places to purchase moonshine. It's located on the edge of Great Smoky Mountains National Park, about eight miles south of Pigeon Forge, home to Dollywood, Dolly Parton's family-focused amusement park. Unlike Dollywood, however, Ole Smoky's target demographic is the 21-and-older crowd. Moonshine is made on site, with free tours available for visitors to learn about the liquor's history and lore. Moonshine samples are on the house. In the bottle room, jars of Ole Smoky sell for $25 each. Branded T-shirts, baseball caps, and glass tumblers are available in the gift shop. Outside the main entrance, in "Mountain Moonshine Holler," there's a rushing manmade brook designed to look like the primo spot for an old-time whiskey maker to set up his still, and rocking chairs that invite visitors to sit a spell and enjoy the live bluegrass band.

FULL THROTTLE

In 2012, Ole Smoky Tennessee Moonshine became the official moonshine of NASCAR's Bristol Motor Speedway, a short-track venue in Bristol, Tennessee, and Charlotte Motor Speedway, a giant motorsports complex in Concord, North Carolina.

Perhaps one of the more unusual origin stories surrounding a modern, aboveboard moonshine operation belongs to Popcorn Sutton's Tennessee White Whiskey. The product is named after Marvin "Popcorn" Sutton, an old moonshiner out of Cocke County, Tennessee, who enjoyed a reputation for making the best booze around. He also had a flair for self-promotion. In 1999, Sutton published a book called *Me and My Likker: The True Story of a Mountain Moonshiner*. A documentary was released the following year, called *This Is the Last Dam Run of Likker I'll Ever Make*. (It was later renamed *The Last One*.) "I just done this so people who buy these videos can see what in the hell a moonshiner has to put up with to make a living," Sutton says in the opening scene. A wizened man with a wiry beard, trademark overalls, and a burning cigarette perpetually dangling from his fingers, Sutton also appeared in *Hillbilly: The Real Story*, a 2008 History Channel documentary.

Enter Jamey Grosser. One night in 2008, he was at home in Northern California watching CNBC. The housing crisis dominated the news, and there was fear of a second Great Depression. In his late 20s at the time, Grosser was in the midst of his own crisis. He'd spent the last several years as a professional motorcycle racer, and was contemplating a career change. The cultural pendulum, he saw, was shifting.

"People were really getting back to basics," Grosser says. "Instead of getting a triple infused apple martini" at a high-end lounge, they were going to a local pub and "buying a Jäger bomb and a beer."

It occurred to Grosser that he might enjoy a career in the liquor business. Not the fancy stuff, whose makers often sponsored his racing events, but moonshine, the booze that fueled the underground economy during the Great Depression, that period of American history which the CNBC reports kept referencing. He booked himself a flight to east Tennessee. "That's one of the last places it was, up in the mountains," Grosser explains.

After landing, Grosser hopped in his Kia rental car and started driving through the hills, stopping at homes and knocking on doors. "How do I learn about it? Who can I talk to?" he asked. "Everybody was like, well, you gotta talk to Popcorn Sutton." That night in his hotel, Grosser did his research. "I typed his name into Google and boom! All this stuff popped up about him. I'm like, he's the most famous un-famous guy I've never heard of." The big news was that Sutton had recently been busted for offering to sell 1,000 gallons of moonshine to a federal agent and was sentenced to 18 months in prison. Grosser tracked Sutton down through his probation officer.

Perhaps it was because Sutton was on house arrest and eager for company that he invited Grosser into his ramshackle home. The two of them talked for hours, Grosser recalls, bonding over their shared love of women and whiskey. When it was time to go, Sutton insisted that Grosser—whom he'd taken to calling "Grocery Boy"—stay overnight. Overnight turned into five days, and Sutton later entrusted Grosser with his moonshine recipe. "I want you to help me," Grosser says Sutton told him. "I don't want this to die with me."

But Grosser would have to do the work without Sutton by his side. Four days before he was to begin serving his prison term,

Sutton got into his green Ford Fairlane and killed himself by inhaling exhaust fumes. He died on March 16, 2009, at the age of 62. It was now up to Grosser to keep Sutton's legend and his liquor alive.

With Hank Williams Jr. and Sutton's wife, Pam, as business partners, Grosser set up shop in Nashville and in 2012 released his first bottles of Popcorn Sutton's Tennessee White Whiskey. In the beginning, the liquor was packaged in Mason jars marked *XXX*, "to honor history," Grosser says. But the vessel has since changed. As Grosser explained, "People have such a stigma about unaged whiskey, that no matter what you sell in a Mason jar, they think it should be ten bucks and it's gonna taste like shit." The crystal-clear whiskey now comes in a tall, matte-black bottle. The tagline: America's Rebel Spirit. "Because that's what Popcorn was," Grosser says, "and what his liquid is."

Recognizing growing consumer interest in the white whiskey category, three of America's biggest whiskey makers, Jim Beam, Maker's Mark, and Jack Daniel's, responded in 2013 by releasing their own white whiskeys. Jim Beam's product is called Jacob's Ghost. (Though because it spends a year in barrel, it doesn't quite qualify as moonshine or new-make whiskey.) Maker's Mark calls its white dog Maker's White. And Jack Daniel's offers Unaged Tennessee Rye. Another development in 2013: Jack Daniel's filed suit against Popcorn Sutton Distilling for trademark infringement, noting that the company's new bottle and label are "confusingly similar" to its own.

What's the best way to enjoy modern moonshine? Many say it's terrific in cocktails, imparting a flavor distinct from other white spirits like tequila and gin, and which vodka can't deliver. On a warm evening on the cusp of summer, in 2013, Tavern Law, a bar and restaurant located in Seattle's Capitol Hill neighborhood across the street from a Ferrari and Maserati dealership, had on its specials board a moonshine cocktail called the 7 Star Cooler. A fruity, pink cocktail, no less, mixed with soda water, lime juice, and

A display at PROOF, in Seattle, Washington, 2013.

strawberry syrup, and served in a highball glass with crushed ice and a basil leaf garnish.

Created by the establishment's tattooed and bespectacled bartender, the drink gets its name from the whiskey it's mixed with, See 7 Stars, a moonshine produced at Batch 206, a craft distillery in Seattle. In 2013, there were nearly 550 craft distilleries nationwide, according to American Distilling Institute president Bill Owens. They're small and tend to be independently owned, producing less than 100,000 gallons of spirit a year. Washington State is home to more than 40 craft distilleries, with about 20 more in the planning and construction phase. At least eight of these small distilleries make a product they market as white whiskey or moonshine. "It's a

MOONSHINE MIXOLOGY

Mixologists at Ba Bar, a Vietnamese restaurant and cocktail bar in Seattle's Capitol Hill neighborhood, use 2bar moonshine to make the Spiked Lee.

Spiked Lee

Ingredients

2 oz. 2bar Spirits Moonshine
2 oz. Bellegems Bruin sour beer
½ oz. beet juice
½ oz. lemon juice

¼ oz. cane syrup
¼ oz. Vietnamese simple syrup (made from shiso leaf and Vietnamese coriander, or rau ram)
14 oz. cranberry juice
Dash of Tabasco
Shiso leaves for garnish

Directions

Place all ingredients in a small Mason jar. Add ice and affix lid to jar. Give to guest to shake.

Recipe courtesy of Ba Bar mixologist Jon Christiansen

renaissance," Owens says, comparing the rise of small distilleries to the craft beer and slow-food movements. "People want things that are homegrown. And what's more homegrown than whiskey and moonshine?"

"Of course, the mixologists go crazy over this stuff. It has flavor. It has character. It's handmade. You can meet the distiller himself. He's a person. It's not coming out of corporate America, owned by a foreign government. Who wants to drink water from Fiji?" he asks, bemoaning the practice of importing from far away what can be tapped and bottled and harvested locally. "There's nothing more American than whiskey."

On top of the trend, Washington Distillers Guild organized its first-ever tasting event, PROOF. It took place on a Saturday, in June 2013, in an industrial space tucked alongside an elevated highway in the city's SoDo (south of downtown) district. The place was packed, with a few hundred drinkers in attendance. Tickets to the evening affair sold out quickly, at $45 apiece, so an afternoon session was added to accommodate the demand. And just as Bill Owens suggested, people seemed genuinely excited for the chance to meet the makers. From one draped table to another they went, sampling spirits conservatively dispensed into shot glasses that had been handed out at the door. Of the 34 distilleries represented at PROOF, 6 of them made unaged whiskey.

Batch 206 was set up near the entrance. Bottles of See 7 Stars were prominently on display alongside the distillery's vodka and gin. Master distiller Berle "Rusty" Figgins was on hand. See 7 Stars, he said, gets its name from a colloquial term for powerful shine. To develop the product, Figgins and distillery owner Jeff Steichen, who owned Seattle's iconic music venue the Showbox before getting into the liquor business, built a moonshine-tasting library. The winner was White Dog Whiskey, from Buffalo Trace, a distillery in Frankfort, Kentucky, that focuses on bourbon. It was a logical connection, as Figgins often describes moonshine as bourbon without the barrel.

At the table next to Batch 206 was 2bar Spirits, maker of moonshine and vodka and a soon-to-be-released bourbon. Distillery founder Nathan Kaiser proudly offered samples to a steady flow of visitors. Originally from Texas, Kaiser, who has a degree in microbiology, opened the distillery in October 2012 in a small garage-like space at a strip mall on Seattle's west side. It's equipped not with a gleaming copper still, which is the centerpiece investment made by many of Kaiser's counterparts, but with modestly sized steel drums that appear jerry-rigged, giving the distillery a kind of backwoods do-it-yourself vibe. There's also a certain hipness to the place: Attached to the side of each of the distillery's fermenting tanks—the 275-gallon plastic containers that hold soupy mash for up to two weeks as the grain converts its sugars to alcohol—is a black-and-white photograph of a female country music star. There's June Cash, Connie Smith, Patsy Cline, and Dolly Parton, who sang about the dark side of alcohol in the 1971 tune "Daddy's Moonshine Still."

Across the room from 2bar at PROOF was Carbon Glacier, a distillery that makes its home south of Seattle in rural Wilkeson, Washington, population 477, near majestic Mount Rainier. Carbon Glacier's clear Moose Shine Whiskey is made from a mash of corn, oats, and barley. It's a grain formulation traditionally used as feed for farm animals, explained the distillery's burly young rep, a culinary-school graduate whose earlobes were stretched by a pair of dime-sized plugs. To a guest, he said that he started making moonshine when he was nine years old; that air bubbles formed by shaking a bottle of liquor, called the bead, reveal vital information ("The smaller they are and the faster they go away, the higher the proof"); and that "good moonshine," when lit with a match, should burn blue ("If there's methanol or acetone [in it] it will burn yellow or green"). Open and on display at his table was a straw-lined case that held a glass jug of Moose Shine, with an illustration of a heavily antlered moose on the label, alongside a small wooden barrel. It's a package designed for the enthusiast who wants to play around with aging his whiskey at home.

"It's cute," said a guy wearing pristine white sneakers, a gold chain, and sunglasses on top of his head. He identified himself as a bartender. "But you gotta sexy it up. Put it in a different bottle. You can get a different market."

"Sexy" is a look embraced by white-whiskey makers hoping to cultivate an image more highbrow than hayseed. Heaven Hill, a large-scale commercial distiller and marketer out of Bardstown, Kentucky, released in 2013 its Trybox series of new-make whiskeys—unaged versions of the distillery's Evan Williams straight bourbon and Rittenhouse Rye. Packaged in squat, 750-milliliter bottles with gunmetal and steel blue labels, the product looks sophisticated on a dramatically backlit bar. Its name comes from the contraption distillers use to catch and taste-test whiskey as it comes off the still. The target audience is whiskey aficionados eager to try their favorite spirit in its purest form, before any interaction with the barrel.

Small distillers have taken a similar approach. Brian Ellison, of Death's Door distillery, in Middleton, Wisconsin, is one of them. Bottles of his wheat-based White Whisky are tall and slim, with a sleek white-on-black label. Ellison says the whole endeavor was a fluke, initiated by his Chicago distributor who urged him to make whiskey in addition to the vodka and gin he was already doing. Ellison's response: "I can't afford whiskey." Buying barrels in which to store the spirit, and waiting years for the whiskey to age, was too much for the young business to bear. It's a problem faced by many small distilleries, and the reason so many of them focus at first on unaged products. But the distributor kept at him. If Ellison wasn't ready to go the distance with whiskey, how about making an unaged version? He said he'd buy 50 cases.

It was an enticement Ellison couldn't resist. "It was February and I was making no money and I said, 'I'll have it ready by Friday.'" In three days, all 50 cases—300 bottles—were sold, and the distributor asked for 50 cases more. "People are totally intrigued by it," Ellison says. But, he adds, they don't necessarily understand what the product is. What's more, he prefers to distinguish his white whiskey from so-called moonshine, with its reputation as a foul-tasting, potentially lethal, beverage. When Lincoln Restaurant, in Washington, D.C., started mixing Death's Door White Whisky with ginger syrup, fresh lemon, and orange bitters and calling the cocktail Honest Abe's Moonshine, Ellison cringed a little at the name ("Well, we're really not moonshine," he wanted to say) but decided it was better for business to keep any contrariness to himself.

The moonshine name has been good for business in Brooklyn, where the white whiskey coming out of Colin Spoelman's Kings County Distillery *is* moonshine, in the sense that it's made in the tradition of the spirit, from a blend of 80% corn and 20% malted barley. On Saturday afternoons, Spoelman leads tours of the distillery, which is housed in the Brooklyn Navy Yard's paymaster building, where workers once came at the end of each week to collect their wages. The two-story red brick structure, built in 1899, stands just beyond the Navy Yard's Sands Street entrance. Decommissioned in 1966, the yard is now an industrial complex, home to small businesses like Kings County Distillery and bigger ones too, among them Steiner Studios, where HBO shoots *Boardwalk Empire*, a series set in Prohibition-era Atlantic City, New Jersey.

On an August weekend in 2013, a handful of participants gathered on the distillery's front steps. Spoelman, who was dressed in skinny jeans and a white polo shirt, began the tour by sharing the distillery's origin story before moving on to the basics of western Pennsylvania's Revolutionary-era Whiskey Rebellion, the result of protests against the country's tax on distilled spirits. He then pointed out the irony of locating his business inside the Navy Yard: In the late 1800s, soldiers and policemen marched from the yard and into the surrounding neighborhood in raids that destroyed whiskey stills and confiscated liquor from the homes of the Irish immigrants who distilled whiskey in defiance of U.S. law prohibiting the operation of unlicensed, untaxed stills.

It was sunny outside. Spoelman led visitors to a modest cornfield planted alongside the distillery, which he hopes will yield 50 pounds of corn by the end of the growing season, enough to produce one batch, or a hundred 375-milliliter bottles, of whiskey. It's a small complement to the three tons of cracked corn delivered to the distillery every three to four weeks. But there's something special about seeing the fresh green blades that push through the soil and the baby ears of corn that sprout from the plant's sturdy

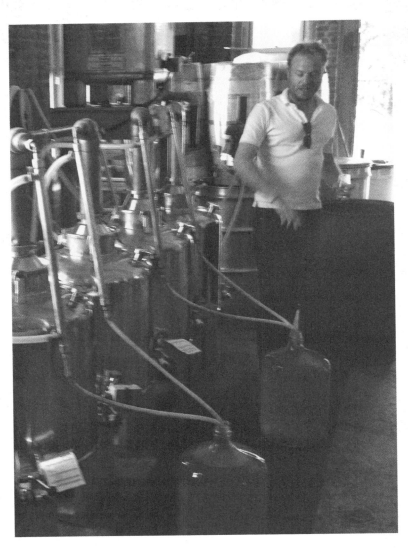

Colin Spoelman of Kings County Distillery, in Brooklyn, shows visitors how the distillery makes its moonshine.

Kings County Distillery grows its own corn. This crop is enough to make a hundred 375-milliliter bottles of white whiskey.

stalks. For hundreds of years, this traditional American grain is what's gone into countless jars of whiskey. Corn juice, people call it.

Next, Spoelman ushered his guests into the distillery, entering through the building's back door. Here he showed off the little eight-gallon still used in his Williamsburg apartment to make his first batch of moonshine. It looks like a pair of stainless steel buckets stacked one on top of the other with a long pipe sticking out from the top. As he spoke, the sweet smell of fermenting and cooked corn lingered in the air. Along the wall, five small metal stills in a row pumped out a cloudy first run of spirit, and in the center of the loft-like space stood two onion-shaped copper stills made to order in northern Scotland. When they're up and running, they'll replace the quintet of little stills and produce 30 gallons of spirit a day, some to be bottled straight away, as moonshine, while a portion of the distillate will be placed in five-gallon wooden barrels and carried to an upstairs storage room where it will age into bourbon.

Still, it's moonshine that remains the distillery's top seller, its calling card, and the product for which it's best known. Yet Spoelman now thinks *white whiskey* is the more appropriate name for the spirit. "It's more descriptive," he says. A "real" backwoods moonshine recipe would undoubtedly contain sugar, he notes, but it's not an ingredient in the whiskey made by Kings County Distillery. "When we got started, *moonshine* was what people understood. When you said 'moonshine,' they got it. If you said 'white whiskey,' it didn't mean anything to them."

That's starting to change as interest in American whiskey increases. In 2013, sales of straight American whiskey, which includes bourbon and Tennessee whiskey, grew by 4.4%, and sales of rye whiskey increased by about 47%. That growth, says Spoelman, is likely to translate into a greater appreciation and demand for "good" white whiskey, bourbon's unaged variant. "Whether or not we call it moonshine, that actually may fade away," Spoelman says. "Now the moonshiners are urban moonshiners. They're people who are chefs; people who are home brewers; and people who are interested in it not for profit." He adds, "I think the moonshiner in the woods really does not exist in the way that it exists in the public's imagination." That's something, he believes, that died with bootlegger Maggie Bailey, who passed away in Harlan County, Kentucky, in 2005, at the age of 101.

MAKING MOUNTAIN DEW

Go away, go away, darlin' Corey
Stop hanging around my bed.
Bad liquor has ruined my body,
Pretty women gone to my head.

—"Darling Corey," traditional (recorded by Buell Kazee in
1927 and the Weavers in 1955)

At 9:30 on a Saturday morning in mid-July 2013, eleven students gather in front of the tasting bar at Dark Corner Distillery in downtown Greenville, South Carolina. Head distiller John Wilcox does the pouring, doling out samples of clear corn whiskey into a line of disposable plastic shot cups. "Tiny sips," he advises. "Pace yourselves." There will be more drinking to come. The distillery's monthly moonshine-making course is five hours long.

The class attracts a diverse student body. Enrolled in a summer session is an Indiana dad and his college-senior daughter in town for a drop-off at Furman University, and a pair of German expats from the purchasing department of a nearby diesel-engine production facility. A pharmacist from Knoxville, Tennessee, interested in "medicinal mixology" is there, along with a South Carolina tourism blogger and a home brewer from Columbus, Ohio, whose wife signed him up for the class as a birthday present.

Wilcox, the teacher, is dressed for class in baggy camouflage shorts, a black button-down Dickies shirt, a brown knit cap on his prematurely bald head, and toe shoes, which make him look as if he is wearing gloves on his feet. After shots at the bar, he leads the group to a makeshift lecture hall set up in the distillery's basement, and students take their seats alongside sacks of grain and pallets of flattened cardboard packing boxes, under track lights that have been dimmed in advance of a PowerPoint presentation.

With one blue, bulleted screen after the next, the slide deck could easily be a buzzkill, but Wilcox keeps the class lively, beginning with his perfunctory announcement about emergency exits and the potential that exists for an explosion when working with high-proof spirits. "In case of a fire, we will hang out," he says, drinking whiskey to pass the time "until we are rescued or die."

He gives a brief history lesson that touches on government taxation, the Whiskey Rebellion, and South Carolina legislation that allowed Dark Corner to become one of six distilleries to open in the state since 2011. After that, he explains how whiskey is made.

First, malt the grain. This means moistening the grain, be it corn, wheat, barley, whatever you want. (At Corsair Distillery, in Nashville, they're making whiskey from quinoa, Wilcox says.) This causes the grain to germinate, or sprout. Many distilleries, including Dark Corner, purchase grain that's already been malted.

After that, dry the malted grain and grind it into a coarse meal. Then mix the grain with water and boil to make the mash. Stir the thick, soupy blend with a mash stick or paddle to keep the grain from sticking to the bottom of the pot and scalding. When the mash has cooled, add yeast. Leave it to ferment in barrels or tanks. This liquid is what distillers call beer. Fermentation takes about three to four days, depending on ambient temperature. Keep an eye on it. Once, says Wilcox, uttering a reference that betrays his annual trips to the psychotropic-infused Burning Man art festival in the Nevada desert, "I was not being a good daddy to my yeast babies and I let them party too hard." He wound up with a mash that had the acrid scent of movie-theater popcorn. Finally, add the beer to the still. Heat and wait for the spirit to trickle forth.

Why is the distiller's beer called "beer" when it's clearly not the beer most people are familiar with, someone wants to know. Wilcox explains that beer and whiskey are not dissimilar. Both are made from malted grain, yeast, and water. Essentially, whiskey is distilled beer, minus the hops and fizziness. Wilcox apprenticed at Denali Brewing Company in Alaska, which is where he is from, but when it comes to distilling, he is entirely self-taught, having learned to make whiskey by "a lot of reading, a lot of gnashing the teeth, and a lot of trial and error." His approach has been successful: Dark Corner Distillery moonshine has racked up several industry awards, including a gold medal in the moonshine category at American Distilling Institute's 2013 Artisan American Spirits competition.

To demonstrate the distiller's art, Wilcox hands out a second round of plastic shot cups into which he pours from an unlabeled bottle a thimble's worth of clear liquid.

"Holy crap!" says the home brewer from Ohio as he watches the Indiana dad seated at the folding table in front of him chug his sample like a shot of vodka. "That guy drank the whole thing." The brewer, it should be noted, took one sip and coughed violently, as if he were about to choke. He saved his chugging for the pint of bottled water Wilcox gave out as a chaser.

Normally, knocking back a shot would be unremarkable. That's just how it's done. But this taste test is meant to be instructive: What Wilcox gave his students was a blend of the first two parts of the distillate to come off the still, the foreshots and heads. Both contain methyl alcohol, which can be deadly if consumed in large quantities, as well as acetone, the stuff of nail-polish remover. Wilcox wasn't trying to kill anyone; heads are safe in small amounts, though they can lead to a massive hangover. Typically, distillers collect and redistill this portion of the run. It's called making cuts.

Next, Wilcox pours from a bottle of tails, or feints. This is the end of the run, the last bit of liquid that drips off the rig. While some

THE PEACH BLOSSOM

Ingredients
1½ oz. Dark Corner Distillery Carolina Peach Shine
½ oz. Dark Corner Distillery Honeysuckle Shine
1 oz. white grape juice
½ oz. cranberry juice
1 peach wedge

Directions
Combine all ingredients except for the peach wedge in a rocks glass. Stir to mix evenly. Fill the glass with crushed ice and garnish with a peach wedge.

Recipe courtesy of Dark Corner Distillery

Pitcher by pitcher, distiller Paul Fulmer fills Dark Corner Distillery's copper pot still.

of this liquid will be saved and redistilled on a second run to add character to the whiskey, it tastes unpleasant on its own. Wilcox describes it as "mop water." This time around, the Indiana dad is more cautious. Also taking it slow is the Knoxville pharmacist. He grimaces, and pronounces the liquid "cardboardy," which seems generous. The South Carolina blogger has a harsher assessment. "I can see sobriety in my future," she says.

The class moves upstairs to Dark Corner's distilling room, a small glass-enclosed area on the selling floor, which is thick with a pungent aroma, like corn bread baking in an oven. In one corner of the room stands a pair of 55-gallon stainless steel pots filled with a hot, bubbling mash of corn, red wheat, and barley. In the opposite corner are 55-gallon plastic and steel drums in which mash has been left to cool and ferment. The liquid in one vessel looks cloudy. In another, a thick head, or cap, of corn has formed on the surface. As fermentation continues, the cap will drop to the bottom of the barrel. In a third drum rests a milky mixture with golden globules of corn oil floating on top. This is the beer that Wilcox talked about earlier. Tastes are offered. It's tangy and sharp.

Shaped like a bird, with a round body, a small head, and a pipe, called a lyne arm, which looks like a long, skinny beak, Dark Corner's copper pot still takes pride of place in the center of the room. The lyne arm connects the still to the condenser, which is a wooden barrel filled with cold water and lined with a copper coil, or worm. Students take turns dipping a plastic pitcher into the barrel of beer and pouring the oily liquid into the mouth of the still. The still then heats the beer, and steam rises into its head. Vapor moves through the lyne arm before traveling into the condenser, where it's shocked by cool water and turned back into liquid as it flows through the worm. Eventually, this liquid trickles from a narrow spigot toward the bottom of the condenser. It's clear as water. This is the beer strip, the first run at extracting alcohol. The liquid will then be distilled a second time. Some whiskey makers insist on triple distillation. (Those Xs on a jug of backwoods moonshine are said to stand for the number of times the liquor's been distilled.) With

For its distinctive shape, the coil lining the side of this cold-water condenser barrel is called the "worm." As steam passes through the worm, it turns back into liquid.

each turn through the still, flavor decreases and alcohol level increases. Do this enough times and you end up with vodka.

No matter what type of still is used, the transformation from liquid to steam and back to liquid is the same. The scientific principles are basic: Water boils at 212 degrees Fahrenheit. Methyl alcohol, or methanol, boils at 151 degrees Fahrenheit, and ethyl alcohol, or ethanol, boils at 173 degrees Fahrenheit. During distillation, methyl alcohol is first to vaporize. Methanol steam rises, and after hitting the condenser and turning back into liquid, it's the first alcohol to come off the still. Discarding this part of the run is a crucial step in distilling. Knowing how much of the run to dump is part of the distiller's art. So is knowing when to start collecting what's known as "the heart" of the run, which is the finest part of the distillate. Modern distillers have tools to help determine when to make cuts. But they also make decisions based on smell and taste, just as moonshiners did in the old days. Wilcox says he samples the distillate every five minutes.

"How do your taste buds survive this?" a student asks.

They haven't, Wilcox says. A fan of spicy food, he can no longer gauge the heat.

When it's time to proof the spirit students gather round as Wilcox wheels into the center of the room another 55-gallon drum. This one's blue, plastic, filled to the brim with clear whiskey, nearly 148 proof, or 74% alcohol by volume. "Just don't light a match near me," Wilcox says.

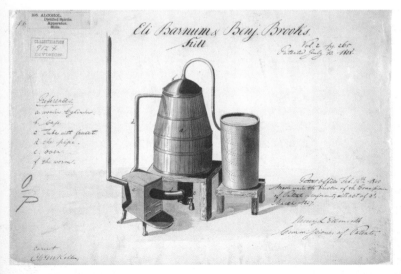

Still design patent, Eli Barnum and Benjamin Brooks, 1808.

MOONSHINE STILLS OVER TIME

Traditionally, moonshine has been made in copper pot stills. Sometimes called turnip stills, these devices get their name from the distinctive rounded shape of the boiler. They're the kinds of whiskey stills used by America's Scots-Irish settlers and their early descendants, and they're still used by distillers today. Over the years, however, moonshiners developed other types of stills with the goal of making more whiskey in less time than pot stills.

Blackpot submarine stills were popularized in the 1920s. Shaped like rectangles with rounded ends, these stills were made with planks of wood and sheets of metal. They were much bigger than the copper pot still, and could produce about 800 gallons of whiskey at a time. They also had the advantage of offering one-stop whiskey making: Mash could be made directly in the still and heated when ready. According to the Blue Ridge Institute in Ferrum, Virginia, "a typical mash recipe for an 800-gallon still includes 50 pounds of rye meal, 50 pounds of barley meal, 800 pounds of sugar, and water."

Steam stills were the biggest of all, though less common. In this type of still, seen in the early 1900s, steam was sent directly into the mash, causing the liquid to boil and give off alcohol vapors which then pass through a worm, where they're turned back into liquid. The mash doesn't have to be stirred, and it doesn't scorch since the heat is under the water boiler, not the mash pot.

Today, reflux stills are common. Unlike copper pot stills, which require distillers to run the liquor through the still two to three times to get the desired alcohol content, reflux stills can complete a batch of whiskey in a single run. That's because the still is shaped like a column and filled with either metal plates or some kind of packing material, be it glass beads or wads of metal, similar to scouring pads. This creates more surface area and allows the vapors to rise and trickle back down, then rise again. These multiple distillations result in a higher-proof spirit.

At this high a proof, the alcohol is highly flammable. It's what he warned students about four hours ago when the class began. "This is corn whiskey in the raw," Wilcox adds. "I've had some real honest-to-God illegal whiskey and it tastes a lot like this." To be sure, the Dark Corner region still has its share of moonshiners. When asked about them, though, Wilcox acts as if he hasn't heard the question. Sometimes these whiskey makers show up in class with an eye toward going legal. A few have even pulled out Mason jars filled with homemade liquor in the middle of a session. Wilcox won't tolerate it. He's got a reputation to uphold and a government license to protect, and enough to worry about with all the federal requirements he has to follow for proofing, bottling, and labeling his liquor.

That's the trinity on which the last hour of the moonshine-making course is focused. First comes proofing. To turn the liquid into something that the average person would find potable, dilution is essential. Wilcox wants to bring that 148 proof whiskey in the blue plastic drum down to 100 proof, or 50% alcohol. To do it, he sets onto the concrete floor a white plastic bucket into which he transfers a portion of the spirit. He then adds to it bottled spring water, mixing the liquid with a long-handled metal paddle. Next, he pours a sampling of the liquid into a foot-tall graduated cylinder into which he inserts a tool called a hydrometer. The alcohol content of the liquid is determined by how deep or how high the instrument sits in the liquid.

"I say you leave the water out," one students cracks. But Wilcox keeps going, adding water and testing, then adding more water and testing again. "We do this over and over again until we get perfection," he says. The home brewer from Ohio offers assistance in the form of an iPhone app called Distillers Toolbox, designed to calculate the volume of water needed to bring a spirit down to the desired proof. Back in the day, distillers didn't even have thermometers.

Finally, Wilcox gets the whiskey where he wants it. Because the federal government assesses taxes by proof gallon, correct measurements are critical. Since 1991, the federal tax has been set

Postcard, "A typical moonshine still in the heart of the mountains."

at $13.50 per proof gallon, which means that for each standard-sized 750-milliliter bottle of 100-proof spirit, a distiller owes the federal government about $2.70. The amount changes depending on the percent of alcohol in the spirit. State taxes vary.

Now it's time for bottling. Wilcox pours the proofed spirit into an automated filling contraption called the Enolmatic before demonstrating how to properly place each bottle on a labeling machine that's activated by depressing a foot pedal. He shows students how to apply a plastic collar to the cap of the bottle *just so* and how to seal it with a heat gun. When the whole operation is up and running, it verges on the classic candy conveyer belt scene from *I Love Lucy*, but instead of Lucy and Ethel being overwhelmed by chocolates, it's the German engineers and the Ohio home brewer and the Indiana dad-and-daughter duo going head-to-head with the Enolmatic: Fill the bottle; pull it off at just the right moment; then *fast!*— hook the next empty bottle up to the machine. Repeat. By the time each student has filled a bottle, sealed it, and added the government-approved label, they're cradling those bottles as if they were babies.

THE OUTLAW LEWIS REDMOND

South Carolina's upcountry region was home to one of the country's most notorious 19th-century moonshiners. His name was Lewis Redmond. In 1877, in retaliation for the arrest of another local moonshiner, Redmond and his associates invaded a revenue officer's home in the middle of the night. The officer wasn't there. But instead of leaving, the Redmond crew proceeded to insult and curse the man's wife and to threaten his life. For this act, Redmond wasn't apprehended, but two of the invaders were. They were tried the following spring at the United States District Court, in Greenville, where their attorney asserted that before the Civil War, making whiskey was common among mountain folk. "It was not wrong then," he said, "and it can't be such a great crime now." For his part, the judge instructed jurors to consider whether "Redmond law or the laws of the government" should rule the region. The defendants were convicted, but the jury asked that the men receive merciful treatment. Three years later, Redmond was convicted for the murder of a U.S. deputy marshal who was on his trail for moonshining, and sentenced to 10 years in prison, serving much of his time at a federal penitentiary in Albany, New York. After just 22 months, however, Redmond was released, having been pardoned by President Chester A. Arthur. He returned to making liquor, this time for a government-run distillery in Walhalla, South Carolina, where he was put in charge of a special whiskey called Redmond's Hand Mash.

Class is officially over. Wilcox dismisses his students, sending them back to the tasting bar. Now, students sample the whole range of spirits produced at Dark Corner distillery, including gin, absinthe, and Lewis Redmond Carolina bourbon whiskey, named after a notorious South Carolina moonshiner who lived and worked in the region nearly 150 years earlier, making whiskey on a still that in all likelihood bore a remarkable resemblance to the one used today by Dark Corner.

MOONSHINE IN POP CULTURE

Let me tell the story, I can tell it all
About the mountain boy who ran
    illegal alcohol.
His daddy made the whiskey, son,
    he drove the load.
When his engine roared, they called
    the highway Thunder Road.

—Jack Marshall and Robert Mitchum,
"The Ballad of Thunder Road"
(performed by Robert Mitchum as the theme song
to the 1958 feature film *Thunder Road*)

On the 10th floor of an Art Deco office building south of Wall Street in New York City's Financial District—home to the production office of the Discovery Channel docudrama *Moonshiners*—executive producer Chris Tetens rolls a chair into an edit room the size of a small walk-in closet. On a monitor, he watches two men in South Carolina agonize over a fouled-up batch of strawberry brandy, using their bare hands to scoop sludge from the metal drum the fruit was left to ferment in, then flinging it onto the grass in frustration. In the next scene, an earnest goofball new to liquor making buys a custom-made copper still from a front-porch artisan who's missing several teeth. Cut to the guy driving his pickup along a sinuous country road with the still in the truck bed. Tetens, tall, bald, and slender, with polka-dot socks and a five-o'clock shadow, leans forward in his chair and wheels closer to the screen. "A thin sheet of cardboard is all he has to conceal it," he says in dramatic television-announcer style, and just like that, the box pulls loose in the wind to expose the apparatus, a tease to viewers that the man's in danger of getting pulled over on suspicion of brewing illegal hooch.

"Are you ready to send it?" Tetens asks his editor when she pauses the action. It's only a scratch VO, meaning the final voiceover has yet to be recorded, and subtitles must still be added in a few sections to make up for the double whammy of southern accents, mumbled. But otherwise, the show looks good. "Let's send it," Tetens says. With that, he wheels his chair out the door and down a narrow passageway to another edit room, where he'll scrutinize another rough cut. One episode down—almost—and 12 more to go until the premiere of season 3, just six weeks away.

The *Moonshiners* season 2 finale pulled in nearly 4 million viewers, making it the most-watched cable television program in its Wednesday evening time slot. Since its 2011 debut, the series has evolved. That year, it focused on Tim Smith and his still hand, Tickle, moonshiners from southern Virginia's Pittsylvania County, one county away from Franklin, a moonshining stronghold for more than a century. In 2012, the series brought on new moonshiners, including Josh and Bill from South Carolina—the pair making strawberry brandy—and Jim Tom, an old moonshiner and master of copper still construction, based in North Carolina.

From the beginning, skeptics have complained that the show's moonshiners are inauthentic, that these guys surely would have been arrested had they really been making non-tax-paid liquor. For its part, the Virginia Department of Alcoholic Beverage Control issued in 2011 a news release in which it called out the show for what it characterized as a "false depiction of moonshine manufacturing, distribution, and/or transportation."

But Tetens, a New Jersey native who previously worked on the Discovery Channel show *Secretly Pregnant* and is currently producing a feature-length documentary about the New Orleans criminal justice system, insists his moonshiners are the real deal. When the show was getting started, he spent months with Tim Smith in Virginia, working to build trust and develop the kind of relationship that would allow him and a small production crew to document Smith's illicit business. For the first month, however, Tetens was convinced that Smith had him pegged as an undercover agent.

"He wouldn't meet with me. Then he *would* meet with me. And then he would set up these little tasks, like, well, 'Bring me a six-pack. Bring me a bottle of Jim Beam.' I'm like, all right already. He was milking me," Tetens says of the testing period Smith put him through. "And then finally, somewhere, he said, 'Well, I'll do this but I *won't* do this. I'll show you this but I *won't* show you this. Well, maybe I can do a thing where I'm showing my son how to do it.' Slowly, he warmed up to it. It took a long time."

Tetens is not exaggerating. Initially, producers budgeted four weeks to shoot material for three episodes. In the end, it took six months, shooting with a crew that was often no more than four people strong, in 12-hour stretches, following Smith to secret locations hidden in the hillsides. "It was like a camping trip," Tetens says of his time spent with Smith.

Since then, Smith has realized his goal of going legal, bottling and selling Tim Smith's Climax Moonshine, named for the town where he's chief of the volunteer fire department, and based on a corn, rye, and barley recipe handed down from his father, who passed away not long before Smith was approached to do the show. Tetens thinks it was the death of Smith's father that played into his decision to participate. Matt Ostrom, the executive producer who came up with the idea for the series and hired Tetens as his right-hand man, agrees.

"Tim was always taught: 'You never talk about moonshining, and if you do, it's in a low voice. And you certainly never talk to strangers about it,'" Ostrom explained from the nerve center of Magilla Entertainment a few floors above the company's warren of edit suites. With his father gone, however, Smith was free to open up. Says Tetens: "He really wanted to show the world that [his father] had the greatest recipe." A television show—if it performed well—would be the perfect vehicle for Smith to fast-track his entrepreneurial dream.

It was a challenging concept, *Moonshiners*. How do you make a weekly 60-minute show about an illegal activity and not put your subjects, and yourself, in jeopardy? At first, Ostrom thought the outlaw route would present too many obstacles, so he decided to focus instead on licensed moonshine makers, many of whom were just beginning to set up shop back in 2010 when he was pitching the idea to the network. But that approach had its own set of problems, he learned, after scouting at least a dozen locations. "A legal distillery is not the most compelling thing. It's not like people on boats hunting alligators or fighting giant seas," he says, referring to the kinds of dramatic situations that are the hallmarks of reality television, and the stuff that keeps viewers coming back for more. "It's literally: Water boils. It's science. So it gets a little sleepy," he explained. "And I think that's what's so great about Tim. He took us into the woods."

Moonshiners holds the distinction of being the first reality television series to focus on illicit liquor making. But it doesn't mark the first time moonshine's turned up in film or television. In fact, the moonshine business has been fodder for many a story line. In an episode of the 1960s CBS series *The Beverly Hillbillies*, about a southern mountain family that moves to California after striking it rich when oil is discovered on their land, Granny Clampett stands beside her mansion's "cee-ment pond" and stirs a pot of corn mash. She calls the brew "spring tonic." When she takes a sip, her facial contortions—raised eyebrows and strained neck muscles—convey the drink's potency. The booze is so powerful, in fact, that it sends her into a spontaneous acrobatic flip. "Water! I gotta have water!" Granny says, then dives into the swimming pool to get it. In another episode, when Clampett family banker Mr. Drysdale comes down with the flu, Granny delivers to his bedside a jug of "Possum Ridge Penicillin."

Moonshine also made guest appearances in *The Andy Griffith Show*. Set in fictional Mayberry, North Carolina, the series aired from 1960 to 1968. In season 1, episode 17, "Alcohol and Old Lace," spinster sisters Miss Jennifer and Miss Clarabelle make whiskey and sell it from their backyard, along with fresh-cut floral bouquets as decoys. It's Sheriff Andy Taylor's son, little Opie (a young Ron Howard), who turns his dad and Deputy Barney Fife (played by Don Knotts) on to the ladies' ruse.

"Ain't they pretty, Pa?" Opie asks about the flowers when he stops by the jail to exchange the funny-smelling Mason jar they came in for a proper vase to give to his teacher. He tells his dad that the women have a flower-making machine.

"What'd it look like?" Andy asks.

"Well, it's a big, round copper pot with a fire under it, and there's a pipe that curls round and round, like this," the boy says, motioning with a stubby finger, "and runs into a little bucket."

A bit player in *The Beverly Hillbillies* and *The Andy Griffith Show*, moonshine had a starring role in *The Dukes of Hazzard*.

Moonshine made an appearance in a 1961 episode of *The Andy Griffith Show* when Sheriff Taylor and Deputy Fife uncovered a still operated by a pair of spinster sisters.

MOONSHINE MUSIC

Over the years, moonshine has been a favorite subject of singers and songwriters. Here are 10 titles to add to your playlist:

"Mississippi Mud," by Hank Williams III (2002)
This one's a party song. Over a catchy fiddle track, Williams sings about a guy who likes to get "pure drunk" drinkin' moonshine from the jug.

"Revenooer Man," by Alan Jackson (1999)
Originally recorded by George Jones, in 1963, this tune's sung from the perspective of a gun-toting revenue agent boasting about his ability to track down moonshiners.

"Tear My Stillhouse Down," by Gillian Welch (1996)
A moonshiner laments a life darkened by alcohol, and makes a final wish: Destroy the copper kettle where he "made that evil stuff."

"Copperhead Road," by Steve Earle (1988)
The title track off Earle's 1988 album tells of a vet fresh from Vietnam who turns the family's moonshining tradition on its head when he decides to traffic in marijuana instead.

"Kentucky Moonshine," by Pure Prairie League (1975)
This easy-breezy country-rock love song seems meant for whiling away the afternoon on a front porch, sharing a Mason jar with a special friend.

"Daddy's Moonshine Still," by Dolly Parton (1971)
A bootleggin' daddy, liquor-runnin' brothers, and a long-suffering mother: These are the characters who populate Parton's country narrative, which manages to lay bare the painful reality of one family's life in the whiskey business in a surprisingly upbeat tempo.

"Franklin County Moonshine," by Jean Shepard (1965)

A woman puts her foot down when it comes to her husband's moonshining ways. It's all he seems to care about it, and the stress of it's turning her black hair gray. This liquor lament is capped with a yodeled call to arms.

"Chug-a-Lug," by Roger Miller (1964)

Here's a humorous song about a young man's first encounter with moonshine whiskey. "Makes you want to holler 'hi-dee-ho!'" the narrator says. Toby Keith's 2010 album *Bullets in the Gun* includes a live cover of Miller's Top 10 hit.

"White Lightning," by George Jones (1959)

Soon after country singer George Jones released this rockabilly-inflected tune, it rose to Number 1 on the country music charts, making it his first hit single.

"Moonshine Kate," by Moonshine Kate and Fiddlin' John Carson (circa 1928)

Between 1928 and 1930, father-daughter team Rosa Lee and John Carson performed a series of comedic moonshine-themed song-skits, including "Moonshine Kate," in which Kate acts the part of a moonshiner's offspring. "Do they make whiskey to sell?" she's asked about her parents. Her answer: "They don't make it to give away."

On the air from 1979 to 1985, the show's main characters were Bo and Luke Duke, Georgia cousins played by Tom Wopat and John Schneider, and moonshine-making Uncle Jesse. Each episode featured the Duke boys speeding around in General Lee, their 1969 Dodge Charger with a hood painted to resemble the Confederate flag and an air horn programmed to play the opening notes of "Dixie,"

MOONSHINE'S BIG-SCREEN DEBUT

Red Margaret, Moonshiner was one of the first movies about bootleg liquor. Released in 1913, the silent, black-and-white romance starred Pauline Bush as a moonshiner in love with a government agent (Murdock MacQuarrie), and a young Lon Chaney in a pre–*Hunchback of Notre Dame* role as her wannabe suitor. According to the Internet Movie Database, the film may have been reissued in 1916 as *Moonshine Blood*. It is now believed to be lost.

as they attempted to outrun crooked Hazzard County Commissioner Boss Hogg, and Sheriff Rosco Coltrane. Country superstar Waylon Jennings was the show's omniscient narrator, "The Balladeer." He performed the show's theme song, too. In 1980, "Good Ol' Boys" rose to the top of *Billboard*'s country music singles chart.

The series was an outgrowth of the 1975 film *Moonrunners*, which opens with brothers Bobby Lee and Grady, played by James Mitchum (son of screen legend Robert), getting pulled over on suspicion of transporting moonshine, then segues into a bar fight at the Boar's Nest, which lands Bobby Lee in jail. When he gets out, he makes his way to see his Uncle Jesse, who's known to make the best moonshine around. Lately, however, sales have been slow, and a raid by revenue agents sets him back. Uncle Jesse scoffs when a rival tries to buy him out and blend Jesse's high-quality supply with what he considers to be an inferior product.

"Am I to compromise all the things I've done my whole life for a few extra dollars, just to help a little man think he's a big man?" Uncle Jesse asks his nephews when they prevail upon him to cooperate. "Boys, it's a matter of principle."

Based on the real-life story of North Carolina moonshiner Jerry Rushing, the film performed respectably at the box office. Nevertheless, it was panned by *Variety*. "Aside from some hairy cross-country auto chases, the picture has little to recommend it," the reviewer wrote, describing James Mitchum's portrayal of Grady as "wooden."

With car chases, criminality, and a built-in good-guy-versus-bad-guy story line, moonshining was an irresistible subject for filmmakers. In 1973, Burt Reynolds starred in *White Lightning* as Gator McKlusky, a moonshiner released from an Arkansas prison in exchange for working undercover to break up a moonshine ring. The film's sequel, *Gator*, came out in 1976. Before that, in 1970, Alan Alda and Richard Widmark starred in *The Moonshine War*, based on the Elmore Leonard novel of the same name.

The moonshiner genre also had its share of B-movies. The poster for Roger Corman's 1977 *Moonshine County Express* amped up the tits-and-ass factor. It shows the film's male lead, John Saxon, flanked by two buxom women, both bare chested beneath their overalls, one with a rifle over her shoulder, the other suggestively lifting a crock of whiskey to her lips. The tagline: *He drives the fastest car in the state! She makes the best shine! They make it every night.* Maureen McCormick, in a post–*Brady Bunch* role, sheds her Marcia Brady image and appears in the film as a moonshiner's daughter.

The film that set the standard for all moonshine movies that came after it, however, is the cult favorite *Thunder Road*. Released in 1958, the movie starred bad boy Robert Mitchum as Lucas

"THUNDER ROAD" WAS ONLY A PRACTICE RUN.
THIS IS THE REAL THING.

You take a load of 200 proof corn likker through a police roadblock at 100 miles an hour and if you ain't a dead man, you're a moonrunner.

LIKE FATHER...
LIKE SON...
BIG JIM MITCHUM
GEAR-GRINDING,
TIRE-SCREAMING,
HOT-RODDING
BOOTLEG SHINE!

"MOONRUNNERS"

ROBERT B. CLARK presents "MOONRUNNERS" starring JAMES MITCHUM
KIEL MARTIN and ARTHUR HUNNICUT · Balladeer: WAYLON JENNINGS
Executive Producer ROBERT B. CLARK · Written and Directed by GY WALDRON

PG | PARENTAL GUIDANCE SUGGESTED

United Artists

Viewers have the 1973 film *Moonrunners* to thank for the TV series *Dukes of Hazzard* and for the Jessica Simpson movie that came after that.

Doolin, a veteran who's come home to Harlan County, Kentucky, after serving in the Korean War and promptly gets to work hauling whiskey for his moonshining father. The role of Robin Doolin, Luke's younger brother, was first offered to Elvis Presley. But Presley's fee was beyond the film's budget, so the role went instead to Mitchum's look-alike son, James.

Mitchum wrote the story as well as the movie's theme song, "The Ballad of Thunder Road." The film was perhaps the one project in which he was the most personally invested, and he had plenty of tough-guy street cred with which to inhabit the leading role. Before becoming an actor, he'd led a vagabond's life, riding the rails, hitchhiking, getting sent to jail on a vagrancy charge, and escaping from a chain gang. By 1948, he'd made his mark in show business, but he hadn't totally reformed: Mitchum was busted that year in a sting operation for possession of marijuana and served time behind bars.

It's unclear whether the plot of *Thunder Road* was based on an actual case, but it relied on true-life stories in its depiction of the southern moonshining business. To develop the script, Mitchum and his writing partner, James Atlee Phillips, spent days in Washington, D.C., meeting with officials at the United States Treasury Department, poring over records maintained by the Alcohol and Tobacco Tax Division, and learning about mountain culture by listening to archival recordings of "hillbilly" music at the Library of Congress.

Mitchum next went to Asheville, North Carolina, where the movie would be shot, and requested a meeting with the city's resident Treasury agent, who brought with him to the get-together the man heading up the local Alcoholic Beverage Control board. It was a win for Mitchum, eager as he was to get moonshining culture right. Even the cars used in *Thunder Road* were authentic liquor-hauling vehicles purchased around Asheville from actual bootleggers.

With the film's release, a press packet distributed to theater owners detailed a number of stunts for generating excitement about the picture. They ranged from displaying a "hot rod" outside the theater, to a "Thunder Road Guitar Contest" for young musicians, to a tie-in with local retailers selling men's and boy's apparel. The suggested advertising line: "The Mitchums—Father and Son—Are Terrific Together in 'Thunder Road.' . . . Fathers and Sons Go Terrific Together in Johnson's Clothes!"

Other promotional ideas were far less family-oriented, pushing hard on the illicit activity angle. They included the innocuous—"Set up ordinary steel file cabinets in your lobby, plainly marked 'Secret T-Man File'!" (*T-man* meaning an agent employed by the U.S. Treasury Department to track down moonshiners)—and the downright absurd:

> If there is a regional Internal Revenue Service office in your area, suggest they lend you any captured weapons, ammunition, and other illegal materials or equipment found in the hands of revenue-law violators.

Imagine the modern corollary: arriving to a theatrical screening of *Breaking Bad* to find a lobby display of actual evidence seized at a bust on a meth lab, including the coffee filters, solvents, and packets of over-the-counter allergy and cold medicine used to manufacture the drug.

For years after its release, *Thunder Road* remained a box office favorite, particularly at drive-in movie theaters throughout the southeastern United States, where it consistently managed to generate ticket sales of the five- to six-figure variety. The film's popularity and proven earning power is one reason United Artists held back its release to home video until the late 1980s, a good 25 years after it first appeared in theaters.

Audiences especially loved *Thunder Road*'s epic ending: Mitchum as Lucas Doolin, barreling down a dark, winding road, cigarette dangling from his lips, federal agents on his tail. In the film's final moments, Doolin's car fishtails, his tires burst by spikes. He swerves, and the vehicle flips three times before crashing into an electrical transformer.

As sparks zap the vehicle, with Doolin trapped inside, two agents observe his final moments. "Mountain people. Wild-blooded. Death-foolish," one of them says. "That was Doolin all right. He was a real stampeder."

More than 40 years since the release of *Thunder Road*, audiences continue to be fascinated by moonshining. Discovery Channel's *Moonshiners* proves it. What's different is that the people onscreen aren't acting, and they're in danger of being busted by the law. After the first few shows aired, state agents showed up at Tim Smith's home, eager to use the show as evidence of illegal activity, says producer Tetens. But without catching a moonshiner in the act, there's no way to pursue a case.

How do the moonshiners on the show feel about how they're portrayed? "I think they get a kick out of it," Tetens says. "Moonshining, until we started filming it, has been a really solitary, solo, clandestine activity. And all of a sudden, America loved them for it." In fact, *Moonshiners* did so well in its first two seasons that it spawned a spinoff, *Tickle*, which focuses on the adventures of Smith's often-inebriated sidekick. The show's season premiere brought in 1.91 million viewers.

When they're not shooting the show, the moonshiners make personal appearances at distilleries, parades, festivals, and other events across the country. Tetens sometimes goes with them. "There are some fans who just love them because they're on TV and they're famous," he says of the people they meet on the road. "And there's, like, every fifth person who's a real distilling nerd and wants to get technical with them."

Tetens says that the same focus on craft drives the moonshiners on the show. "They go to bed thinking about it," he says of the men's quest to make top-quality liquor. "It's not just swill. They really care about what they put in. They'll sit there like Talmudic scholars, stroking their beards, talking about it."

EPILOGUE

MOONSHINERS REUNION

I am a young fellow
that never yet was daunted,
And sometimes had money,
but seldom it was wanted,
For robbing for gold it was my own folly,
Paying for good liquor to treat deceitful Molly.
                    Mush ring a ding-a-ra

—"Whiskey, in the Jar," traditional Irish folksong
(recorded by Thin Lizzy in 1972, Metallica in 1998, and
Belle and Sebastian on their 2006 single *The Blues are Still Blue*)

For weeks, Starla Landers hyped the event on Facebook. "Only 20 days left until the Old Moonshiners of Georgia Reunion!!!!! YEAH BOY!!!!!" As the gathering drew near, she posted status updates, asking people from how far away they were traveling to get there (700 miles, said one man) and working on her sales pitch: "BTW, don't forget to order your t shirts so we all match." She promised a day filled with music and raffles and free moonshine tastings, courtesy of the host, Dawsonville Moonshine Distillery.

Landers, who lives in Acworth, had been sharing photos of the distillery on her newly formed Facebook page, Old Moonshiners of Georgia. That's how distillery owner Cheryl Wood found out about the group—her daughter, seeing the tags, asked if she knew this lady who was posting pictures online. Wood did not, and she checked out the page herself. That's how she and Landers connected. Both women are granddaughters of old Georgia moonshiners. "Do it here," Wood offered, when Landers told Wood about her dream to stage a reunion. Landers took her up on it.

By noon on Saturday, July 20, 2013, the Georgia humidity was already bearing down, and Landers, an attractive woman with dark hair, was fussing at a table outside the distillery's front entrance, arranging those T-shirts, pink for ladies, black for men. "Moonshine," the shirts said. "Some of the best times you'll never remember." She wore a pink one with black jeans.

Meanwhile, Jeff Brown & Still Lonesome, a Virginia-based bluegrass band, was the day's headline entertainment, and a few early arrivals sat on red vinyl chairs under a shade tent in the parking lot kitty-corner from the Food Lion supermarket, cooling themselves with paper fans as they watched the young violinist, banjo player, and tall skinny teen on the upright bass warm up.

Retired revenue agent Chester Powell stood near Landers and her T-shirt table, turning for the interested corn farmer next to him the yellowed, brittle plastic pages of a photo album filled with newspaper clippings and photos of moonshine busts he'd had something to do

A display of moonshine-making supplies at Dawsonville Moonshine Distillery, in Georgia.

with after becoming a revenuer in 1966, at the age of 21. Used to be, agents destroyed a whiskey haul by shattering the glass jars it came in, or simply pouring the liquor out, but one of Powell's photos showed him backing up a van to burst and flatten an array of moonshine-filled plastic gallon milk jugs arranged behind the vehicle. Those containers weren't always easy for moonshiners to get their hands on, especially after the government started watching who was buying and selling them, and moonshiners took to recycling. "I know a guy got ten cents a piece for washing those jugs," Powell said.

What drew an old revenuer to a moonshiners get-together? "I wanted to see if there was anybody I knew," Powell said. Months earlier, he'd run into a man he'd help put in jail. "He served seven years," Powell said. "Said it was the best thing that ever happened to him. Went out, got straight. Wife and kids now."

Also at the reunion was 78-year-old Bug Jones. He sat on a concrete bench alongside the distillery, dressed in Liberty overalls and a baseball cap, carrying a wooden cane hand-carved to look as if a copperhead snake had wound its body around the staff. According to Jones, he started making moonshine when he was just 14. By the time he was 20, he worked at a still making thousands of gallons of whiskey a week. "We didn't sell it," Jones said, explaining moonshining's division of labor. "All we done was make it." Someone else was in charge of handling the transactions, and a separate crew took care of distribution. Each day, seven days a week, "from daylight to way after dark," Jones said, he and his fellow still hands were helping to put out 450 gallons a day. Over the years, Jones found work on about 30 stills, one of them so big it ate up sixty 100-pound bags of sugar a day. He got caught a couple times, too. Once, he wound up in jail in neighboring Pickens County. Another time, he ended up with three years probation, but he says he never did time in a federal penitentiary.

Pete Bearden approached and took a seat next to Jones. Known by the nickname Flathead, for the V-8 engine in the 1940 Fords so many whiskey trippers once drove, Bearden, a Dawsonville native, told of his years making moonshine in the woods. He got started in 1964, after graduating from high school, having learned from his dad how to make whiskey at just about the time the IRS was ramping up a new round of enforcement efforts aimed at illicit distillers. Most of their customers were in Atlanta, and Athens. Some of it they sold "to good old racecar drivers," two tractor-trailer loads at a time. "They was into it, too," Bearden said. But he wouldn't name names. Discretion is key in the underground economy.

For Bearden and others like him, there wasn't any shame in moonshining. Faced with limited job opportunities, many people turned to whiskey making. "That was the way of life then," Bearden said. "Ninety percent of the Beardens have done it."

Dwight Bearden shows off one of his first stills.

Indeed, Bearden's cousin Dwight is Dawsonville Moonshine Distillery's head whiskey maker, having learned his trade growing up in the family business. As the other old moonshiners milled about outside telling stories, Dwight Bearden and his cohort "Bullet" Bob Suchke, a handsome man who runs a local sawmill when he isn't making whiskey, were busy showing off the distillery's $125,000 copper pot still, giving guests a behind-the-scenes tour, and explaining how to turn sweet Georgia corn into potent white liquor.

How is the distilling process here different from what people used to do in the woods? someone asked. Bullet Bob was quick to answer. "We're in a much cleaner environment," he said. "There's no dead possum in the mash." When another guest asked him about the thin, hooked ornament stuck in his cap, he implored her to rub it for good luck, and he got a kick out of the reveal: "It's a coon's peter bone," he said. A raccoon's penis bone. Just like the one old Tennessee moonshiner Popcorn Sutton used to wear in his hat.

Meanwhile, in the tasting room, Cheryl Wood passed out little cups of Dawsonville moonshine. What she could not do, however, was make sales. Oh, she was allowed to take money in exchange for jars of moonshine pickles and moonshine jelly and spiral-bound *Cookin' with Moonshine* cookbooks, which includes recipes for Chicken Salad with a Twang, Tipsy Vegetable Soup, and Snookered Strawberry Rhubarb Crisp. And people were free to buy bottles of Mitchum's Thunder Road Bootleggers Style "Barely Legal" BBQ Sauce, and campy BEST JUGS IN TOWN T-shirts with images of XX crocks of whiskey strategically placed on the chest. Yet Georgia law makes it illegal for a distillery to sell alcohol on-site. So Wood sent customers to City Liquor, a converted service station just up the road on Highway 53, with the promise that if they bought a jug of Dawsonville moonshine and came back to the distillery with it, she'd autograph the bottle. People did, and in between pouring more samples and telling the story of her family's whiskey-making heritage, Wood used a black Sharpie to authenticate her product, signing it with her nickname, "Happy" Wood. Bullet Bob was signing, too.

Today, the people of Dawsonville, Georgia, no longer rely on moonshining and whiskey trippin' as a way to make a living, and farming isn't the town's only industry. There's work to be had at Gold Creek Farms, processing chicken; at SleeveCo, producing colorful plastic shrink-seal wraps on jugs for Prestone antifreeze and twin packs of Fischer nuts; and at North Georgia Premium Outlets, selling discounted designer clothes, or serving hot pretzels and pizza at the development's fast-food restaurants. Other businesses based in Dawsonville include sheet-metal fabricator World Wide Manufacturing; Atlanta Motorsports Park, a kind of fast-car-driving country club; and numerous hotels, including Best Western and Comfort Inn, that line Georgia 400, the eight-lane highway that links Dawsonville to Atlanta.

Still, the people of Dawsonville take pride in the past, turning out for moonshiner reunions, the town's Mountain Moonshine Festival, and volunteering at the impressive Georgia Racing Hall of Fame to share with visitors tales of hometown boys, including several whiskey trippers who went on to make a name for themselves in auto sports.

Dawsonville's not the only place in America to celebrate its moonshining roots. And Dawson County's not the only place to claim the title of Moonshine Capital of the World. Franklin County, Virginia, shares the distinction, and it's there, at Ferrum College's Blue Ridge Institute & Museum, that the Blue Ridge Folklife Festival takes place each year. Along with music and mule-jumping demonstrations, ticket holders can see displays of traditional moonshine stills and attend panel discussions featuring retired moonshiners and revenue agents. For those interested in digging deeper into the region's moonshine past, the college holds an extensive collection of photographs and oral histories. Less scholarly but more entertaining moonshine history can be found in Rocky Mount, where Franklin County Historical Society's annual Moonshine Express tour takes the curious for a ride on a vintage bus to meet costumed guides—including one dressed as the diamond-toothed, liquor-car-driving Willie Carter Sharpe of the 1935 Moonshine Conspiracy Trial, who tell the story of the county's involvement in the illicit liquor trade.

Also claiming the Moonshine Capital title is New Straitsville, Ohio. It was here, during the Great Depression, that out-of-work coal miners turned to making whiskey, setting up their stills in abandoned coalmines. It's said that the booze was so good that it came to be called the New Straitsville Special. Since 1970, the town's Main Street has hosted an annual Moonshine Festival, a five-day event held over Memorial Day weekend, complete with carnival rides and tractor pulls, moonshine-themed food, a Miss Moonshine Pageant for girls 15 to 18 years old, and a Little Miss Moonshine contest for girls between 4 and 6. For the duration of the festival, the town grants organizers a permit to operate a moonshine still for demonstration purposes only. No tasting allowed.

Washington, Pennsylvania, a city near Pittsburgh, pays tribute to its role in the nation's liquor history a bit differently. First staged in 2010, the city's Whiskey Rebellion Festival commemorates, well, the Whiskey Rebellion, and for three days in July the city recalls those heady post-Revolution protests against Alexander Hamilton's unpopular whiskey tax. Most of the action unfolds on the Saturday of the festival, with a daylong roster of historical reenactments, including the capture by federal agents of a rebel farmer, and the tarring and feathering of a tax collector. In 2013, the Saturday program attracted upwards of 7,000 people.

Dawsonville leaders are considering their own reenactments to attract more tourism. The city's racing museum and moonshine distillery draw their fair share of visitors, says Mayor James Grogan. Add one more thing for people to do in town, though, and you stand a chance of keeping them there for the day, spending time and money at local businesses. One idea, says Grogan, is to stage a mock moonshiner trial at the old Dawson County courthouse, then haul the prisoner off in a vintage vehicle and lock him up in the Dawson County jail, a two-story red-brick building in the center of town with bars on the second-floor windows. Both buildings are National Historic Landmarks.

One piece that's a definite in Dawsonville's revitalization efforts is the renaming of eight downtown streets in honor of racecar drivers, some of whom had a dual history as whiskey trippers. Among the changes: West 1st Street becomes Raymond Parks Street; West 2nd Street switches to Roy Hall Street; and West 3rd Street will be known as Lloyd Seay Street. East 1st Street belongs to Bill Elliot. He wasn't a moonshiner, but the retired NASCAR champ will forever be known by the lyrical nickname "Awesome Bill from Dawsonville."

The push to rename the streets came out of a study Dawsonville did in conjunction with the University of Georgia, with an eye to attracting tourism dollars. To start the process, says Grogan, the city first had to understand its identity. Surveys were conducted. Public meetings were held. It wasn't hard for residents to name Dawsonville's heart. "We are a moonshine and racing town," said Mayor Grogan. "That is our heritage."

Heritage is what moonshine is all about. Moonshine is tradition. It's family. It's folk art, and people are invested in keeping the art alive. It's what drove Cheryl Wood to open Dawsonville Moonshine Distillery, that desire to give a new generation a taste of her granddad's Georgia corn whiskey. It's the moonshine mystique that has led distillers across the country to embrace this uniquely American liquor. And it's what pushed Starla Landers to connect with old moonshiners through social media. Her Old Moonshiners of Georgia Facebook group has spawned affiliates in Alabama, Oklahoma, Tennessee, and the Carolinas. Moonshine's a fad, some people say. Zoot suits were a fad. So were pet rocks and Rubik's Cubes. None of those can claim moonshine's long and storied place in American history. Plus, you can't catch a buzz off a Rubik's Cube.

NOTES & SOURCES

Prologue: Bangin' in the Woods
Page
12   *heavy with alcohol:* McGee, 758.
12   *"VIII bolls of malt:* MacLean, 20.
13   *nurtured on one's own land:* Kellner, 32.
14   *Many of these early immigrants put down roots first:*
           Webb, 132.
14   *For the worm:* Marshall, 200.
15   *Free served time in jail:* Dabney, 25.

1: "The Pernicious Practice of Distilling" in Early America
Page
16   *"No man ever became suddenly:* Rush, 25.
18   *alcohol content of cider:* Nathan, 35.
18   *per capita consumpton:* LaVallee, LeMay, Yi, 1.
19   *beer was considered safer:* Theobold
19   *confinement in stocks:* Dorchester, 109.
19   *"A maid servant in the ship:* Winthrop, 15.
19   *"Robert Cole:* Dorchester, 110.
19   *"None licensed to sell strong waters:* Ibid., 112.
20   *"We can make liquor to sweeten our lips:* Ibid., 110.
20   *It was part of the social fabric:* Carson, 4.
20   *"Wee have found a waie:* Theobold
20   *"a copper still, old:* Ibid.
20   *the distillery produced brandy:* Brodhead, 358.
20   *leftover slop from brewing beer:* Curtis, 96.
21   *sharply limiting the distillation of grain:* Thomann, 110.
21   *there existed a swift trade:* Carson, 7.
21   *In Boston, distilleries were established on:* Dorchester, 119.
21   *200,000 gallons of rum a year:* Curtis, 97.
21   *annual consumption of rum:* Kurlansky, 95.

21   *"a fitting conjunction of two monstrous evils:* Dorchester, 119.

21   *When Britain imposed the Molasses Act:* Kurlansky, 95.

22   *imposition of the Sugar Act:* Ibid.

22   *his compendium included:* Isaacson, 108-111.

23   *punish by lashing:* Dorchester, 120.

23   *"Resolved, That it be recommended:* Ibid.

23   *daily ration,* Ibid., 121.

23   *"A gill of whiskey:* Ibid., 122.

24   *Pennsylvania passed a law:* Ibid.

25   *"certain extravagant acts:* Rush, 6–7.

25   *The face now becomes flushed:* Ibid.

26   *"The consumption of ardent spirits:* Hamilton

27   *ordered by his doctor:* Chernow, 92.

27   *"War and bloodshed:* Maclay, 386-387.

2: Whiskey Rebels, "Watermelon Armies," and President Washington

Page
29   *Early in the morning:* Findley, 84.

29   *35 men . . . guns, sticks, and clubs:* Neville, 193.

29   *farmers bartered their whiskey:* Brackenridge, 17.

29   *nine cents per gallon:* Hogeland, 69.

30   *drafted petitions:* Findley, 42.

31   *"[We] will consider such persons:"* Brackenridge, 33.

31   *reducing the tax rate:* Syrett

32   *pledge to make life difficult:* Findley, 44.

32   *a group of 12 armed men:* Syrett

32   *bound him to a tree:* Findley, 60.

32   *blood boil:* Ibid., 82.

32   *deserved rougher treatment:* Ibid., 79.

33   *near the glass:* Brackenridge, 41.

33   *a young woman escaped:* Neville, 194.

33   *Five were wounded:* Ibid.

33	*a detachment of 11 military men:* Syrett
33	*a series of signals:* Neville, 194.
33	*lead to the groin:* Brackenridge, 49.
33	*broke into Neville's cellar:* Ibid.
34	*Neville wrote a letter:* Neville, 193.
35	*delivered a serious threat:* The American Presidency Project
35	*On August 14:* Brackenridge, 65.
35	*a tree-studded bluff:* Findley, 113.
35	*The outdoor gathering attracted:* Ibid.
36	*"Liberty and no excise:* Ibid., 115.
36	*a committee of 60 people:* Ibid., 116.
36	*met in Pittsburgh:* Ibid., 117.
36	*owed by farmer-distillers:* Ibid., 118.
36	*an anonymous incitement:* Ibid., 119.
37	*"Brothers, you must not think to frighten us:* Brackenridge, 267.
37	*70 armed infantrymen:* Findley, 122.
37	*"That in the opinion of this committee:* Ibid., 128.
38	*the commissioners recommended:* Crackel
38	*12,950 men:* Ibid.
38	*On Tuesday, September 30, 1794:* Ibid.
38	*Upon reaching Bedford:* Hogeland, 217.
38	*"Dreadful Night:* Brackenridge, 316.
39	*on Christmas morning:* Ibid., 330.
39	*from Blackhorse Tavern to the city jail:* Ibid.
39	*two men were convicted:* Hogeland, 238.
39	*John Mitchell:* Brackenridge, 323.
39	*The other convicted man:* "The Whiskey Rebellion," last modified September 4, 2012, http://www.ttb.gov/public_info/whiskey_rebellion.shtml.
39	*Some people paid cash:* http://www.discus.org/heritage/distillery/ accessed June 28, 2013, excerpted from Dennis J. Pogue and Esther C. White, *George Washington's Gristmill at Mount Vernon*

40   *$332.64 in taxes:* Pogue, 125.

40   *a heftier bill:* E-mail message to author from Esther C. White, Ph.D., Director of Historic Preservation & Research, George Washington's Mount Vernon, May 17, 2013.

41   *reimbursed Neville $6,172.88:* Felton, 59.

3: War on Whiskey: Taxing Liquor and Defying the Law in the 1800s

Page

44   *about 2,000 stills:* Downard, xxii.

44   *"More water is then added:* "An Essay on the Importance and the Best Mode of Converting Grain into Spirit, as a Means of Promoting the Wealth and Prosperity of the Western Country" (Lexington, KY: W. W. Worsley's Book-Selling, Book-Binding and Book-Printing Establishment, 1823), 6.

44   *stinging sensation:* Ibid., 15.

47   *flat tax of $50 and a per-gallon tax of 20 cents:* Joseph J. Lewis, introduction to *Report of the Commissioner of Internal Revenue of the Operations of the Internal Revenue System for the Year Ended June 30, 1863* (Washington: Government Printing Office, 1863), 66.

47   *$1 per gallon:* Ibid., 3.

47   *"perpetually at war:* Ibid.

47   *$2 a gallon:* Downard, Appendix VII.

47   *"Since the 1st of January last:* "Frauds on the Government," *New York Times*, May 24, 1865.

48   *agents descended upon the Port Richmond:* "A Whisky Riot," *New York Times*, October 4, 1867.

49   *December 3, 1869:* "The Whiskey War; Military Expedition to 'Irishtown,'" *New York Times*, December 4, 1869.

51   *"Here ye seed to-day:* "The Campaign in Irishtown," *Brooklyn Eagle*, December 4, 1869.

51   *"We have seen detectives:* "An Armed Levy of Taxes," *Brooklyn Eagle*, November 3, 1870.

53   *a secret investigation:* Rives

53   *more than $3 million:* "Whiskey Ring," The Columbia
      Encyclopedia, 6th ed. 2012. Encyclopedia.com. (April 7, 2013),
      http://www.encyclopedia.com/doc/1E1-WhiskRngR.html.

53   *"The extent of these frauds would startle belief:* Green B.
      Raum, introduction to *Annual Report of the Commissioner
      of the Internal Revenue for the Fiscal Year Ended June 30,
      1877* (Washington: Government Printing Office, 1877),
      http://www.irs.gov/pub/irs-soi/1877dbfullar.pdf.

54   *"It is like, they say:* "The 'Moonshiners' Plea,"
      New York Times, July 19, 1878.

54   *In 1877, a team of 11 revenue agents:* Green B. Raum,
      introduction to *Annual Report of the Commissioner of the
      Internal Revenue for the Fiscal Year Ended June 30, 1878*
      (Washington: Government Printing Office, 1878) iv, http://
      www.irs.gov/pub/irs-soi/1878dbfullar.pdf.

55   *subdued with a pistol whipping:* "Driven Away By
      Moonshiners," *New York Times,* February 22, 1880

55   *April 25, 1886:* "A Fight with Moonshiners,"
      New York Times, April 27, 1886.

55   *"This deed scarcely created a ripple:* Raum, introduction, v.

56   *To find moonshiners:* Atkinson, 34-35.

56   *followed the footprints of sheep:* Ibid., 59–60.

56   *"He is six foot two:* Ibid., 89–90.

57   *"They will join the company of moonshiners:* "Georgia
      Moonshiners Enlist," *New York Times,* June 18, 1898.

57   *"I have made whisky since my old man died:* "A Female
      Moonshiner," *New York Times,* March 18, 1893.

57   *"Nancy the Moonshiner:* "Nancy, the Moonshiner," *Brooklyn
      Eagle,* February 2, 1896.

59   *"Men do not make whiskey in secret:* Kephart, 87.

Page

62   *Protests led to the law's repeal in 1856:* Kelly Bouchard, "When Maine Went Dry," *Portland Press Herald*, October 2, 2011.

63   *"Give to the Winds Thy Fears:"* Burns, 103.

63   *"low-down," sawdust-on-the-floor tavern:* Thompson, Tuttle, Rives, and Willard, 73, 84.

63   *175-pound woman:* http://www.britannica.com/EBchecked/topic/404216/Carry-Nation.

64   *the law of the land in 26 states:* "Full Text of the Wickersham Commission Report on Prohibition," *New York Times*, January 21, 1931.

65   *"Good-bye, John:"* "Billy Sunday Speeds Barleycorn to Grave," *New York Times*, January 17, 1920.

65   *"white moonshine whisky":* "'Hard' Soda in Pittsburgh," *New York Times*, March 12, 1924.

66   *supplied top-shelf whiskey:* Burns, 207.

66   *toxic substances:* Burns, 218.

66   *28-year-old farmer:* Vaughan, 966-967.

67   *"evident stupefying or knockout effects of this liquor":* "The Menace of 'Moonshine' Whiskey," *The Journal of the American Medical Association*, November 10, 1923, doi: 10.1001/jama.1923.02650190041017.

67   *blindness and death for 27 people:* "Lay Five More Deaths to Wood Alcohol," *New York Times*, February 17, 1922.

67   *"poisonous Christmas liquor":* "Nine Killed Here by Christmas Rum," *New York Times*, December 27, 1922.

67   *"gaze upon the body . . . as a moral example":* "Poison Rum in N.Y. Christmas Takes 8 Lives," *Chicago Daily Tribune*, December 27, 1922.

67   *Polish immigrant:* "Woman Goes to Trial for Death By Poison Rum," *Chicago Daily Tribune*, March 12, 1924.

67   *"coroner's cocktails":* "Figures Show Hooch Toll Rise,

Plamondon Says," *Chicago Daily Tribune,*
September 18, 1922.

67   *death toll from poison alcohol:* "Poison Rum Toll Continues
      to Rise," *New York Times,* January 1, 1927.

67   *"A flood of poison liquor:* "Wood Alcohol Kills Nine Here in
      Two Days," *New York Times,* June 7, 1930.

69   *provided the bulk of illicit alcohol:* "Full Text of the
      Wickersham Report on Prohibition," *New York Times,*
      January 21, 1931.

69   *could now command $22:* Kellner, 104.

69   *"more than this number":* "Full Text of the Wickersham
      Commission Report on Prohibition," *New York Times,*
      January 21, 1931.

69   *"elaborate still":* "Elaborate Whisky Still Discovered
      in Boston Home of Harvard Professor," *San Francisco
      Chronicle,* April 30, 1921.

69   *"two two-gallon jugs of moonshine":* "Twins Are Full of
      Moonshine," *Los Angeles Times,* July 31, 1921.

70   *"like the roar of surf":* "Police Led to Still by Queer Noise,"
      Los Angeles Times, April 11, 1924.

70   *"Baby Moonshiner":* "Boy of Ten Runs Still; Is Nabbed," *Los
      Angeles Times,* November 10, 1922.

70   *"jackass brandy":* "Law Flouted in Oregon,"
      New York Times, March 22, 1926.

70   *"the ancient ways:* "Pacific Coast, Too, Has Its 'Rum Rows';
      No Dryer than East," *New York Times,* March 22, 1926.

70   *Air, sunlight and pure water . . . moonshine is made":* Roy
      A. Haynes, "Slow Death Lurks in Most Moonshine,"
      New York Times, July 25, 1923.

71   *"booze dens":* Orville Dwyer, "320 Seized in Gang Raids,"
      Chicago Daily Tribune, June 15, 1925.

71   *big-time operator:* Kellner, 111.

71   *Upon his release:* "Full Text of the Wickersham Commission
      Report on Prohibition," *New York Times,* January 21, 1931.

71   *"A thorough inquiry . . . enforcement of other laws":* "Full
            Text of the Wickersham Commission Report on Prohibition,"
            New York Times, January 21, 1931.

72   *"In one county . . . illicit liquor":* Frederick C. Dezendorf,
            Wickersham Commission Report, 1075.

73   *"preposterous and untrue":* "Dry Bureau Lawyer Asked to
            Apologize," *Washington Post*, February 24, 1931.

73   *5:32½ p.m.:* "Final Action at Capital: President Proclaims
            the Nation's New Policy as Utah Ratifies," *New York Times*,
            December 6, 1933.

5: Moonshine on Trial

Page

74   *"The trial was extraordinary:* Anderson, 13.

75   *transported his prisoner:* "U.S. Indictment Cites Officials In
            Liquor Plot," *The Washington Post*, February 8, 1935.

75   *emergency brake:* Greer, 35.

77   *"In the fall of 1928:* Ibid., 24.

77   *more than 200 witnesses:* "35 Indictments May Be Result of
            Liquor Quiz," *Washington Post*, January 23, 1935.

77   *protection money to Lee:* J. R. Linweaver, "Harrisonburg's
            Liquor Inquiry To Be Resumed," *Washington Post*, January
            20, 1935.

77   *3,000 pages of transcripts:* "U.S. Indictment Cites Officials in
            Liquor Plot," *Washington Post*, February 8, 1935.

78   *29-year-old lawman:* Charles D. Thompson, 226.

78   *remained free on $5,000 bond:* "Officials Deny Guilt; Post
            Liquor Plot Bail," *Washington Post*, February 9, 1935.

78   *"overt acts":* J. R. Linweaver, "Harrisonburg's Liquor Inquiry
            To Be Resumed," *Washington Post*, January 20, 1935.

78   *Nearly every farm:* Author interview with Roddy Moore,
            Director, Blue Ridge Institute & Museum at Ferrum College,
            May 10, 2013.

79   *77 distilleries:* Thompson, 15.

79   *flour-sack dresses:* Ibid., 21.

79   *"He is a grand-nephew of Robert E. Lee:* Greer, 66.

80   *"granny money":* Charles D. Thompson, 39.

81   *blamed his legal troubles:* Greer, 328.

81   *On Day 7:* Ibid., 159.

81   *Bondurant went on to testify:* "Shooting of 2 By Sheriff Told at Liquor Trial," *Washington Post,* May 1, 1935.

82   *The numbers were astronomical:* Greer, 202.

82   *"Exciting days of the pre-repeal years:* Ibid., 205.

82   *testimony of transporter Clarence Mays:* Ibid., 242.

83   *A handwritten note:* Ibid., 424.

83   *"diamond-studded teeth:* "U.S. Indictment Cites Officials in Liquor Plot," *Washington Post,* February 8, 1935.

83   *By her own account:* Greer, 411.

83   *the government's 165th witness:* Ibid., 422.

83   *Wearing white shoes and a hat:* Ibid., 401.

83   *Operation Lightning Strike:* Chris Kahn, "Taking Aim at Moonshine," *The Southeast Missourian,* September 8, 2001.

85   *145,000 gallons of whiskey:* Greer, 417.

85   *piloted liquor cars for 27 people:* Ibid.

85   *dates with Jeff Richards:* Ibid., 419.

85   *"Down this mountain highway:* "Mountain Men Aid U.S. Smash Moonshine Ring," *Miami Daily News,* November 19, 1934.

85   *He was asked to go to Roanoke:* Taylor and Modlin, 217.

86   *What is the wettest section in the U.S.A.:* Anderson, 12.

86   *"'the little moonshiner' . . . 'big makers'":* Taylor and Modlin, 220.

86   *"It was the excitement got me:* Ibid., 222.

86   *"They wanted to go along with me:* Ibid.

87   *"founded in political prejudice:* "Liquor Plot Jury Frees 3, Convicts 20," *Washington Post,* July 2, 1935.

87   *returned to Franklin County:* Charles D. Thompson, 228.

6: "Death Defying Ding-Dong Daddies From the Realm of Speed:" Moonshine and the Birth of NASCAR

Unless otherwise noted, quotes from Junior Johnson come from an interview with the author.

Page

89   *A story passed down over the decades:* Paul Hemphill, "Where Are You, Lloyd Seay?" *New York Times*, November 12, 1970.

89   *November 12, 1938:* "Like the Movies—Rescued as Car Bursts into Flames," *Atlanta Constitution*, November 12, 1938.

89   *two cars wrecked and another in flames:* "Seay is Winner of Auto Event," *Atlanta Constitution*, November 12, 1938.

89   *"the sensation of the race:* Ibid.

89   *Seay had been arrested:* "Woman Remanded as Liquor Dealer," *Atlanta Constitution*, May 14, 1938.

89   *"death defying . . . realm of speed:* "Lakewood Racers Open 2-Day Event," *Atlanta Constitution*, December 31, 1939.

91   *"the hottest stock-car driver in the land:* "Atlanta Racer, Leay [sic], Favored at Langhorne," *Atlanta Constitution*, July 13, 1941.

91   *Allentown fairgrounds:* "Lloyd Seay Wins Race at Allentown," *Atlanta Constitution*, May 31, 1941.

91   *set a course record:* "Daytona Race Won by Seay in New Mark," *Atlanta Constitution*, August 25, 1941.

91   *"completely dominated the field:* Ibid.

91   *races in pastures and cornfields:* Author interview with Gordon Pirkle, Georgia Racing Hall of Fame.

91   *50 turns around the oval:* Malcolm Davis, "Lloyd Seay Tops Field in Labor Day Races," *Atlanta Constitution*, September 2, 1941.

91   *flecked with rust-colored dirt:* Ibid.

91   *After taking the championship:* "Race Driver Killed," *Atlanta Constitution*, September 3, 1941.

93   *"I wouldn't get out:* "Racer Lloyd Seay Shot to Death in Disagreement with Cousin," *Atlanta Constitution*, September 3, 1941.

93   *"jumped on Lloyd and hit him with his fist:* Ibid.

93   *"Lloyd Seay, lead-footed mountain boy:* Ibid.

93   *unlucky 13:* Ibid.

93   *It was later estimated:* Ed Hinton, "The Legend: Lloyd Seay Was the Young Sport's Brightest Star Until He Was Gunned Down," *Sports Illustrated Presents: 50 Years of NASCAR 1948–1998*, January 28, 1998, 50.

94   *running away . . . in 1928:* Neal Thompson, 16.

94   *invested his earnings:* Ibid., 47.

94   *"the racing team:* Ibid.

94   *Battle of the Bulge:* Ibid., 158.

95   *"some of the more notorious racketeers:* "Don't Make it a Rat Race," *Atlanta Constitution*, August 31, 1945.

95   *"bootlegger sweepstakes:* Keeler McCartney, "5 Labor Day Lakewood Auto Racers Possess Lengthy Police Records," *Atlanta Constitution*, August 31, 1945.

95   *stealing six tons of sugar:* Ibid.

95   *"It will be a shocking display of bad taste:* "Don't Make it a Rat Race," *Atlanta Constitution*, August 31, 1945.

95   *"These hoodlums:* "Tires, Rumrunners, and Races," *Atlanta Constitution*, September 2, 1945.

95   *On race day:* "Lakewood Race Goes on Over Mayor's Protest," *Atlanta Constitution*, September 4, 1945.

96   *"Reckless" Roy Hall won:* Ibid.

96   *Ed Bagley was arrested:* Ibid.

96   *"Young Demon of the Highways:* "Police Admit Hall is Demon at Wheel," *Atlanta Constitution*, September 5, 1939.

96   *"outspeeding the law:* Ibid.

96   *a genius at the wheel:* Ibid.

96   *apparent suicide:* "Ed Bagley, Auto Racer, Found Shot to Death," *Atlanta Constitution*, September 11, 1945.

97   *one-year prison term:* Neal Thompson, 175.

97   *benefit race:* Bob Bowen, "2 Drivers Hurt, Brogdon Takes Charity Race," *Atlanta Constitution*, November 3, 1941.

97   *December 14, 1947:* Neal Thompson, 230.

97   *customizing engines:* Author interview with Gordon Pirkle, Georgia Racing Hall of Fame.

97   *February 15, 1948:* Neal Thompson: 245.

98   *hauling moonshine in a 1940 Ford:* Donovan, 26.

100   *22 cases of moonshine:* "Biographical Conversations with Junior Johnson," UNCTV, originally air date May 7, 2012.

100   *$10 a gallon:* Tom Wolfe, "The Last American Hero is Junior Johnson. Yes!" *Esquire*, March 1965.

100   *just below the windows:* "Biographical Conversations with Junior Johnson," UNCTV, original air date May 7, 2012.

101   *Not once was Johnson nabbed:* Ibid.

101   *"I was 16, barefooted:* Ed Hinton, "The Twelve Greatest Drivers: Junior Johnson," *Sports Illustrated Presents: 50 Years of NASCAR, 1948–1998*, January 28, 1998, 90

102   *He crashed:* Busey.

104   *"manufacturing non-tax-paid whiskey:* "Junior Johnson is Pardoned for Moonshining," *Los Angeles Times*, January 13, 1986.

104   *"I just got aggravated with it:* "The Twelve Greatest Drivers: Junior Johnson," *Sports Illustrated Presents: 50 Years of NASCAR, 1948–1998*, January 28, 1998, 90.

104   *38 drivers:* Ed Hinton, "The Twelve Greatest Drivers," *Sports Illustrated Presents: 50 Years of NASCAR, 1948–1998*, January 28, 1998, 90.

104   *President Ronald Reagan pardoned Johnson:* "Junior Johnson Pardoned for Moonshining," *Los Angeles Times*, January 13, 1986.

105   *He's honored:* Ibid.

105   *"He contributed money and stuff:* http://sports.espn. go.com/rpm/nascar/cup/columns/story?columnist=hinton_ ed&id=5309089.

7: "Popskull Crackdown"

Page

107   *"a persistent search . . . operators:* United States Treasury Department, *Annual Report for the Fiscal Year Ended June 30, 1957* (Washington, D.C.: U.S. Government Printing Office), 18.

107   *"unprecedented:* Licensed Beverage Industries (1955), 9.

107   *36 million gallons:* Ibid., 10.

107   *more than a quarter of all distilled spirits:* Ibid., 5.

107   *"The moonshine problem:* Ibid., 6.

108   *"popskull crackdown:* Sterling E. Soderlind, "Popskull Crackdown," *Wall Street Journal*, September 21, 1956.

110   *to report on a daily basis:* Philip Warden, "Watch Chicago Sugar Firms in Drive on Stills," *Chicago Daily Tribune*, May 12, 1957.

110   *"container pinch:* "Moonshine by the Squirt Latest Bootlegging Fad," *Hartford Courant*, February 9, 1961.

110   *"plastic bags . . . trash dumps:* Ibid.

110   *10 pounds of sugar:* Philip Warden, "Watch Chicago Sugar Firms in Drive on Stills," *Chicago Daily Tribune*, May 12, 1957.

110   *prices ran between $14 and $18:* Sterling E. Soderlind, "Popskull Crackdown," *Wall Street Journal*, September 21, 1956.

110   *roadside shacks:* Licensed Beverage Industries (1951), 27.

110   *federal tax on distilled spirits:* "Historical Tax Rates," Alcohol and Tobacco Tax and Trade Bureau, http://www.ttb.gov/tobacco/94a01_4.shtml.

110   *$1.75 and $2.50:* Sterling E. Soderlind, "Popskull Crackdown," *Wall Street Journal*, September 21, 1956.

111   *"devil's water:* Ralph K. Polad, "Moonshine in the Kitchen,"
       Jerusalem Post, January 14, 1955.

111   *"white lightning:* "Diplomats in Libya Resort to Moonshine,"
       Los Angeles Times, March 31, 1974.

111   *"tastes like . . . after a party:* Peter Shapiro, "A Staggering
       Capacity: Treasury Agents (Not Revenuers, Please) Go After
       Moonshiners, but the Output Remains Little Changed," *Wall
       Street Journal*, August 21, 1973.

111   *27 people:* Don Robinson, "A Report on a Billion-Dollar
       Racket: The New Bootleg Barons are Robbing You," *Los
       Angeles Times*, March 13, 1960.

112   *"Man, do you think I'm crazy:* "Moonshiners Even Shun
       Drinking Own Firewater," *Hartford Courant*,
       February 8, 1963.

112   *dosed their mash:* Paul Coates, "Whisky is Risky," *Los
       Angeles Times*, May 30, 1966.

112   *convulsions and delirium:* "Moonshine Can Be Deadly, U.S.
       Agents Warn," *Spartanburg Herald–Journal*, August 7, 1966.

112   *Poison Moonshine Publicity Program:* United States
       Treasury Department, *Annual Report 1961* (Washington,
       D.C.: U.S. Government Printing Office, 1961), 38.

112   *"Ladies and gentlemen:* Paul Coates, "Whisky is Risky," *Los
       Angeles Times*, May 30, 1966.

116   *"Hey, gang:* Ibid.

116   *In the Carolinas:* Jim Holland, "Moonshine Can Be Deadly, U.S.
       Agents Warn," *Spartanburg Herald–Journal*, August 7, 1966.

117   *serious health consequences:* James T. Wooten, "Moonshine
       trade 'Ain't in the Best of Health,'" *New York Times*,
       December 1, 1970.

117   *"unremitting pressure:* U.S. Treasury Department, *Annual
       Report, Nineteen Sixty-Seven* (Washington, D.C.: U.S.
       Government Printing Office, 1967), 36.

117   *"almost complete elimination:* Ibid.

117   *$2.4 million:* Ibid.

117 *Operation Dry-Up:* Ibid., 38.

117 *in 1968:* Ibid., 36.

117 *aerial photography:* Peter Shapiro, "A Staggering Capacity: Treasury Agents (Not Revenuers, Please) Go After Moonshiners, but the Output Remains Little Changed," *Wall Street Journal*, August 21, 1973.

117 *heat-seeking device:* James T. Wooten, "Moonshine trade 'Ain't in the Best of Health,'" *New York Times*, December 1, 1970.

117 *"People get a little money:* Ibid.

118 *By 1974:* "Cost of Sugar Sours Moonshine Business," *Hartford Courant*, August 27, 1974.

118 *cash crop:* Helen Dewar, "Modern Trends Killing Moonshine Business," *Washington Post*, September 16, 1974.

118 *"moonshine czars:* Jonathan Kwitny, "Bad Business: Moonshiners in South Find Sales Are Down as their Costs Go Up," *Wall Street Journal*, July 30, 1975.

118 *7,000 gallons of moonshine:* Timothy McNulty, "Factories Lure Distillers from Hills, Moonshiners Still Around, But Old Spirit is Gone," *Chicago Tribune*, March 25, 1979.

118 *"Some of the old-timers:* James Branscome, "Moonshiners Shift from Mash to Pot," *Washington Post*, August 8, 1977.

118 *361 moonshine stills:* Timothy McNulty, "Factories Lure Distillers from Hills, Moonshiners Still Around, But Old Spirit is Gone," *Chicago Tribune*, March 25, 1979.

119 *seizures stood at 7,432:* Ibid.

119 *enforcement of federal liquor laws:* U.S. Treasury Department, Annual Report, Nineteen Sixty-Nine (Washington, D.C.: U.S. Government Printing Office, 1969), 33.

119 *unusual raids:* "Moonshine—Blue Ridge Style: The History and Culture of Untaxed Liquor in the Mountains of Virginia," Blue Ridge Institute & Museum of Ferrum College, http://www.blueridgeinstitute.org/moonshine/the_cat_and_the_mouse.html.

119   *"talkin' trash:* Steve Frazier, "C. Garland Bunting Poses as Fish Peddler, Reels in Lawbreakers," *Wall Street Journal*, September 7, 1982.

120   *"This is the way our county lives:* "Locals Upset About Moonshine Bust in Cocke County," http://www.wate.com/story/23354771/locals-upset-about-moonshine-bust-in-cocke-county, September 5, 2013.

121   *10 years in a prison:* 26 U.S.C. § 5601.

8: Moonshine Renaissance

Unless otherwise noted, this chapter is based on author interviews with distillers and reporting from PROOF, held in Seattle, WA, on July 15, 2013, and Kings County Distillery, Brooklyn, NY, on July 27, 2013.

Page

127   *In a television interview:* untv.org, video uploaded to YouTube on March 10, 2011, http://www.youtube.com/watch?v=pe__x7aefRc.

128   *a strong second in moonshine sales:* Technomic Inc., Trends in Adult Beverage Reports.

140   *sales of straight American whiskey:* Email to the author from Donna Hood Crecca, at Technomic, September 6, 2013.

9: Making Mountain Dew

Unless otherwise noted, this chapter is based on reporting from the August 16, 2013, distilling course held at Dark Corner Distillery, Greenville, SC.

Page

150   *"a typical mash recipe:* "Moonshine—Blue Ridge Style: http://www.blueridgeinstitute.org/moonshine/still%20_types_and_techniques.html.

153   *"It was not wrong then:* "Blockade Whisky Makers," *New York Times*, August 28, 1878.

10: Moonshine in Pop Culture

Unless otherwise noted, this chapter is based on reporting from the
Moonshiners production office and interviews with show
producers, September 23, 2013.

Page

155   *nearly 4 million viewers:* Michael O'Connell, "T.V. Ratings:
'Moonshiners' Finishes Record Discovery Month with
Series Highs," Hollywoodreporter.com, January 31, 2013,
http://www.hollywoodreporter.com/live-feed/tv-ratings-
moonshiners-finishes-record-417377.

158   *"Water! I gotta have water!: The Beverly Hillbillies,*
season and episode unknown, clip uploaded to
YouTube on April 7, 2011, http://www.youtube.com/
watch?v=N9Z5Ti9OEH4.

158   *delivers to his bedside: The Beverly Hillbillies,* season 7,
episode 16, "Problem Bear."

163   *"Aside from some hairy cross country auto chases:* Film
review, "Moonrunners," *Variety,* May 28, 1975.

165   *Before becoming an actor:* Server, 27–31.

165   *To develop the script:* Ibid., 321.

165   *authentic liquor-hauling vehicles:* Ibid., 329.

166   *held back its release:* "Thunder Road" (1958), accessed
September 29, 2013, http://movies.nytimes.com/movie/49836/
Thunder-Road/overview.

Epilogue: Moonshiners Reunion

Unless otherwise noted, this chapter is based on reporting from the Old
Moonshiners of Georgia Reunion, held at the Dawsonville Moonshine
Distillery, Dawsonville, GA, July 20, 2013, and author interviews with
Starla Landers and Dawsonville, GA, mayor James Grogan.

Page

175   *abandoned coalmines:* http://www.heartofhocking.com/
New_Straitsville_Ohio.htm.

175   *In 2013, the Saturday program:* http://www.observer-
       reporter.com/article/20130713/NEWS01/130719742.
176   *Among the changes:* http://www.dawsonadvertiser.com/view/
       full_story_free/23204913/article-Dawsonville-streets-to-be-
       renamed.

SOURCES

Primary Interviews
Dwight Bearden, Pete Bearden, Clinton Chumbley, Lenny Eckstein,
Brian Ellison, Joe Fenten, Berle "Rusty" Figgins, James Grogan,
Jamey Grosser, Donna Hood Crecca, Junior Johnson, Bug Jones,
Paco Joyce, Nathan Kaiser, Allen Katz, Starla Landers, Aline McClure,
Charlie Mincey, Joe Michalek, Roddy Moore, Matt Ostrom, Bill
Owens, Craig Pakish, Gordon Pirkle, Bill Pope, Chester Powell,
Heather Shade, Colin Spoelman, Jeff Steichen, Tommy Stevens, Bob
Suchke, Chris Tetens, Jon Thomas, John Wilcox, and Cheryl Wood.

Print and Online Sources
Jerry L. Alexander, *Where Have All the Moonshiners Gone?* (Seneca,
SC: Jerry L. Alexander, 2006).

The American Presidency Project. "Proclamation: Cessation of
Violence and Obstruction of Justice in Protest of Liquor Laws in
Pennsylvania," August 7, 1794. Accessed http://www.presidency.ucsb.
edu/ws/?pid=65477.

Sherwood Anderson, "City Gangs Enslave Moonshine Mountaineers,"
Liberty, November 2, 1935.

George W. Atkinson, *After the Moonshiners, By One of the Raiders*
(Wheeling, WV: Frew & Campbell, Steam Book and Job Printers, 1881).

Hugh Henry Brackenridge, *History of the Western Insurrection in Western Pennsylvania, Commonly Called the Whiskey Insurrection, 1794* (Pittsburgh: W.S. Haven, 1859).

John Romeyn Brodhead, Edited by E.B. O'Callaghan, *Documents Relative to the Colonial History of the State of New York; Procured in Holland, England and France* (Albany: Weed, Parsons and Company, 1856).

Eric Burns, *The Spirits of America: A Social History of Drinking* (Philadelphia: Temple University Press, 2004).

Gary Busey, NASCAR Media Group, and Speed Channel, *NASCAR Hall of Fame Biography: Junior Johnson* (United States: NASCAR Media Group, 2010), DVD.

Gerald Carson, *The Social History of Bourbon* (Lexington, KY: University of Kentucky Press, 2010).

Ron Chernow, *Alexander Hamilton* (New York: Penguin Books, 2005).

Theodore J. Crackel, ed. "Report of the Commissioners, Appointed by the President of the United States, to Confer with the Insurgents in the Western Counties of Pennsylvania," *The Papers of George Washington Digital Edition* (Charlottesville: University of Virginia Press, Rotunda, 2008).

Wayne Curtis, *And a Bottle of Rum: A History of the New World in Ten Cocktails* (New York: Crown, 2006).

Joseph Earl Dabney, *More Mountain Spirits: The Continuing Chronicle of Moonshine Life and Corn Whiskey, Wines, Ciders & Beers in America's Appalachians* (Fairview, North Carolina: Bright Mountain Books, Inc., 1980).

Brian Donovan, *Hard Driving: The Wendell Scott Story: The Odyssey of NASCAR's First Black Driver* (Hanover, NH: Steerforth Press, 2008).

Daniel Dorchester, *The Liquor Problem in All Ages* (New York: Phillips & Hunt, 1884).

William L. Downard, *Dictionary of the History of the American Brewing and Distilling Industries* (Westport, CT: Greenwood Press, 1980).

Margaret Moore Felton, "General John Neville," (M.A. thesis, University of Pittsburgh, 1932).

William Findley, *History of the Insurrection in the Four Western Counties of Pennsylvania* (Philadelphia: Samuel Harrison Smith, 1796).

Linda June Furr, *Cookin' with Moonshine* (Wever, Iowa: Black Iron Cooking, 2009).

T. Keister Greer, *The Great Moonshine Conspiracy Trial of 1935*, (Rocky Mount, VA: History House Press, 2004).

Alexander Hamilton, "Report Relative to a Provision for the Support of Public Credit," *The Papers of Alexander Hamilton Digital Edition*, ed. Harold C. Syrett (Charlottesville: University of Virginia Press, Rotunda, 2011), accessed February 25, 2013, http://rotunda.upress.virginia.edu/founders/ARHN-01-06-02-0076-0002-0001.

William Hogeland, *The Whiskey Rebellion: George Washington, Alexander Hamilton, and the Frontier Rebels Who Challenged America's Newfound Sovereignty* (New York: Scribner, 2006).

Walter Isaacson, ed. *A Benjamin Franklin Reader* (New York: Simon and Schuster, 2003).

Esther Kellner, *Moonshine: Its History and Folklore* (Indianapolis and New York: The Bobbs-Merrill Company, 1971).

Horace Kephart, *Our Southern Highlanders* (CreateSpace Independent Publishing Platform, 2011).

Mark Kurlansky, *Cod: A Biography of the Fish that Changed the World* (New York: Penguin Books, 1997).

Robin A. LaVallee, M.P.P., Heather A. LeMay, B.A., and Hsiao-ye Yi, Ph.D., "Apparent Per Capita Alcohol Consumption: National, State, and Regional Trends, 1977–2011," National Institute on Alcohol Abuse and Alcoholism: Surveillance Report #97 (2013): http://pubs. niaaa.nih.gov/publications/surveillance97/CONS11.pdf.

Elmore Leonard, *The Moonshine War* (New York: HarperCollins, 1969).

Licensed Beverage Industries, *America's Biggest Tax Leak Getting Bigger* (New York: Licensed Beverage Industries, 1951).

Licensed Beverage Industries, *The Moonshine Racket: A Comprehensive Survey of the Trend in Illegal Distilling* (New York: Licensed Beverage Industries, 1955).

Edgar S. Maclay, ed., *Journal of William Maclay, United States Senator from Pennsylvania, 1789-1791* (New York: D. Appleton and Company, 1890).

Charles MacLean, *Malt Whiskey: The Complete Guide* (London: Mitchell Beazley, 2011).

John Marshall, MD, "Laboratory Notes," in *University of Pennsylvania School of Medicine, University of Pennsylvania Medical Bulletin, Vol. I-XXIII* (Philadelphia: University of Pennsylvania Press, 1890).

Harold McGee, *On Food and Cooking: The Science and Lore of the Kitchen* (New York: Scribner, 2004).

Gavin Nathan, *Historic Taverns of Boston: 370 Years of Tavern History in One Definitive Guide* (Lincoln, NE: iUniverse, 2006).

John Neville, letter to Tench Coxe, 1794, in *Monthly Bulletin of the Carnegie Library of Pittsburgh*, Vols. 15-16.

Dennis Pogue, *Founding Spirits: George Washington and the Beginnings of the American Whiskey Industry* (Buena Vista, VA: Harbour Books, 2011).

Timothy Rives, "Grant, Babcock, and the Whiskey Ring," *Prologue Magazine*, (Fall 2000) http://www.archives.gov/publications/prologue/2000/fall/whiskey-ring-1.html.

Benjamin Rush, MD, *An Inquiry Into the Effects of Ardent Spirits Upon the Human Body and Mind* (Boston: James Loring, 1823).

Lee Server, *Baby, I Don't Care* (New York: St. Martin's Press, 2001).

Harold C. Syrett, ed., *The Papers of Alexander Hamilton Digital Edition*, ed. (Charlottesville: University of Virginia Press, Rotunda, 2011).

Welford Dunaway Taylor and Charles E. Modlin, eds., *Southern Odyssey: Selected Writings by Sherwood Anderson* (University of Georgia Press: Athens, Georgia, 1997).

Mary Miley Theobold, "When Whiskey Was the King of Drink," *Colonial Williamsburg Journal*, Summer 2008, http://www.history.org/Foundation/journal/Summer08/whiskey.cfm.

Gallus Thomann, *Liquor Laws of the United States: Their Spirit and Effect* (New York: The United States Brewers' Association, 1885).

Jerry Thomas, *How to Mix Drinks, or The Bon Vivant's Companion* (New York: Dick & Fitzgerald, 1862).

Charles D. Thompson, Jr., *Spirits of Just Men: Mountaineers, Liquor Bosses, and Lawmen in the Moonshine Capital of the World* (Urbana, Chicago and Springfield: University of Illinois Press, 2011).

Neal Thompson, *Driving with the Devil: Southern Moonshine, Detroit Wheels, and the Birth of NASCAR* (New York: Three Rivers Press, 2006).

Eliza Jane Trimble Thompson, Mary McArthur Thompson Tuttle, Marie Thompson Rives and Frances Elizabeth Willard, *Hillsboro Crusade Sketches and Family Records*, (Cincinnati: Jennings and Graham, 1906).

Warren T. Vaughan, MD, "Lead Poisoning, from Drinking Moonshine Whisky," *The Journal of the American Medical Association* (September 16, 1922), doi:10.1001/jama.1922.26420120001015a.

Jim Webb, *Born Fighting: How the Scots-Irish Shaped America* (New York: Broadway Books, 2004).

John Winthrop, *The History of New England from 1630 to 1649* (Boston: Phelps and Farnham, 1825).

PHOTO & MUSIC CREDITS

Prologue: Bangin' in the Woods

Page 6, *"Good Old Mountain Dew" written by Scott Wiseman & Bascom Lunsford. © 1973 Sony/ATV Music Publishing LLC and Tannen Music Inc. All rights on behalf of Sony/ATV Music Publishing LLC administered by Sony/ATV Music Publishing LLC, 8 Music Square West, Nashville, TN 37203. All rights reserved. Used by permission.*

Page 12, *Library of Congress, Prints & Photographs Division,* LC-USZ62-55058

Page 13, *Library of Congress, Prints & Photographs Division,* LC-USZ62-130290

Chapter 1:
"The Pernicious Practice of Distilling" in Early America

Page 17, *Library of Congress, Prints & Photographs Division,* LC-USZ62-58078

Chapter 2:
Whiskey Rebels, "Watermelon Armies," and President Washington

Page 28, "Copper Kettle (The Pale Moonlight)," words and Music by Albert F. Beddoe. TRO—© 1953 (Renewed), 1961 (Renewed), 1964 (Renewed) Melody Trails, Inc., New York, NY. Used by permission.

Pages 30–31, *Library of Congress, Prints & Photographs Division,* LC-USZ62-75625

Page 34, *Library of Congress, Prints & Photographs Division,* LC-USZ62-54169

Page 40, *Courtesy of Mount Vernon Ladies' Association; Photo by Russ Flint*

Chapter 3:
War on Whiskey: Taxing Liquor and Defying the Law in the 1800s

Page 42, *"Rocky Top" written by Boudleaux & Felice Bryant.
© 1967 House of Bryant Publications, renewed 1995.
All rights reserved.*

Page 46, *Library of Congress, Prints & Photographs Division,
LC-USZ6-1409*

Page 48, *Library of Congress, Prints & Photographs Division,
LC-USZ6-61819*

Page 52, *Library of Congress, Prints & Photographs Division,
LC-USZ6-1411*

Chapter 4:
Prohibition: Rise and Fall, and What Happened In Between

Page 61, *Library of Congress, Prints & Photographs Division,
LC-USZ62-45674*

Page 62, *Library of Congress, LC-USZ62-90543*

Page 65, *National Photo Company Collection, Library of Congress,
Prints & Photographs Division, LC-USZ62-42075*

Page 68, *Library of Congress, Witteman Collection, Prints &
Photographs Division, LC-USZ62-106913*

Page 68, *Library of Congress, Prints & Photographs Collection,
LC-USZ62-12143*

Chapter 5:
Moonshine on Trial

Page 76, *Courtesy of Library of Congress, LC-USZ62-136053*

Page 84, *From author's personal collection*

Chapter 6:
"Death Defying Ding-Dong Daddies from the Realm of Speed":
Moonshine and the Birth of NASCAR

Page 90, *Courtesy of Gordon Pirkle*

Page 92, *Courtesy of Dawson County Chamber of Commerce and Office of Tourism Development*

Page 96, *"Rapid Roy (The Stock Car Boy)," words and Music by Jim Croce. © 1971 (renewed 1999) Time in a Bottle Publishing and Croce Publishing. All rights controlled and administered by EMI April Music Inc. All rights reserved. International copyright secured. Reprinted by permission of Hal Leonard Corporation.*

Page 99, *Library of Congress, Prints & Photographs Division, LC-USZ62-55770*

Page 103, *Ted Van Pelt*

Chapter 7:
"Popskull Crackdown"

Page 109, *Government Comics Collection, University of Nebraska, Lincoln*

Page 113, *South Caroliniana Library*

Pages 114–115, *From author's personal collection*

Page 116, *From author's personal collection*

Chapter 9:
Making Mountain Dew

Page 149, National Archives and Records Administration, ARC 305887

Page 152, *From author's personal collection*

Chapter 10:
Moonshine in Pop Culture

Page 154, *"Ballad of Thunder Road,"* words and Music by Don Raye and Robert Mitchum. © 1958 Universal Music Corp. Copyright renewed. All rights reserved. Reprinted by permission of Hal Leonard Corporation.

Page 159, *CBS Television*

Page 162, *Filmland Favorites, 1915*

Page 164, *From author's personal collection*

All other photos by the author

INDEX

Abshire, Henry, 81
acetaldehyde, 67
Adams, Franklin Pierce, 72
After the Moonshiners
(Atkinson), 56
Alcohol and Tobacco Tax and
Trade Bureau (TTB), 124
Alda, Alan, 163
Altamont-Schenectady
Fairgrounds, 102
American Distilling Institute,
132
Artisan American Spirits
competition, 128, 144
Anderson, James, 39
Anderson, Lynn, 42
Anderson, Sherwood, 74, 84,
85–87
Anderson, Woodrow, 91, 93
Andy Griffith Show, The, 158,
159 *ph*
Anti-Saloon League (ASL), 64
aqua vitae, 12
Arbella, 19
Aristotle, 11
Armstrong, Louis, 112, 116
Art of Making Whiskey, The
(Boucherie), 43 *ph*, 44
Arthur, Chester A., 153
Atkinson, George W., 56–57
Atlanta Film Festival, 10

Ba Bar, 133
Babcock, Orville E., 53
Bagley, Ed, 96
Bailey, Maggie, 123, 141
Bailey, Thomas, 76–77, 78
Baker, Joe, 128
"Ballad of Thunder Road, The"
(Marshall and Mitchum),
154, 165
Bangin' in the Woods, 10, 11
Batch 206, 132, 134
Bearden, Dwight "Punch," 9,
15, 172 ph, 173
Bearden, Pete "Flathead,"
171, 173
Beckett, Edgar A., 78

Beddoe, Frank, 28
beer, 144, 147
Beer and Wine Revenue
Act, 73
Belle and Sebastian, 168
Beverage Tasting Institute
(BTI), 10
Beverly Hillbillies, The, 158
Bininger distillery, 17 *ph*
Blackhorse Tavern, 39
blackpot submarine stills, 150
Blue Ridge Folklife Festival, 174
Blue Ridge Institute &
Museum, 80, 150, 174
Bondurant, Forrest, 81
Bondurant, Jack, 81
Bondurant, Matt, 80
"bootleg turn," 101
bootleggers, 66, 77, 100, 110,
123, 165
bottling, 152
Boucherie, Anthony, 44
bourbon, 45
Bower Hill, 29, 41
Braddock's Field, 34 *ph*
Bridges, Jeff, 102
Bristol Motor Speedway, 129
Bristow, Benjamin H., 53
Brooklyn Brewery, 50
Brooklyn Navy Yard, 49, 50–51,
137
Brooklyn Spirits Trail, 50
Bryant, Felice and Boudleaux,
42
Buffalo Trace, 134
Bunting, C. Garland, 119, 120
Bush, Pauline, 162
Byron, Robert "Red," 97

Capone, Al "Scarface," 70–71
Carbon Glacier, 135
Carson, Fiddlin' John, 161
Carter, Yancey, 57
Catdaddy (brand), 126
catdaddy (term), 14
Chaney, Lon, 162
Charlotte Motor Speedway,
129

Chastain, Jessica, 80
"Chug-a-Lug" (Miller), 161
Civil War, 44–45, 47, 54
Coates, Paul, 112
Cochran, Garland "Bud," 118
cocktails, 10, 131–132, 136.
See also recipes
Cole, Robert, 19
Colonial Americans, 18–27
consumption rates, decline in,
117–118
Continental Congress, 23
"Copper Kettle" (Beddoe), 28
copper pot stills, 39, 41, 150
"Copperhead Road" (Earle),
160
Corman, Roger, 163
Corsair Distillery, 144
Cox, Joe Lane, 7
Coxe, Tench, 34
"Crazy Nancy," 57–59
Croce, Jim, 96
Cundiff, Thomas, 80–81
Currier, Nathanial, 62

Dabney, Joseph Earl, 15
"Daddy's Moonshine Still"
(Parton), 135, 160
Danville Fairgrounds
Speedway, 98
Dark Corner Distillery,
143–144, 146 *ph*, 147, 153
"Darling Corey," 142
Darlington Raceway, 102
Davis, James M., 56–57
Dawson County, Georgia,
7–8, 174
Dawsonville, Georgia, 174,
175–176
Dawsonville Moonshine
Distillery, 7, 9–10, 169, 170
ph, 173–174, 176
Daytona, Florida, 91
Daytona 500, 104
Daytona Beach, Florida, 97
Death's Door distillery, 136
Denali Brewing Company, 144
denatured alcohol, 66

Devens, R. M., 31 *ph*
Dezendorf, Frederick C., 72
Distilled Spirits Council of the
    United States, 41
distilling
    handbook for, 43 *ph*
    in Mount Vernon, 39 *ph*,
        40–41
    process of, 11–12, 12 *ph*, 144,
        147, 148 *ph*, 149, 151–152
    tax on, 47
Dorchester, Daniel, 21
"Dreadful Night," 38–39
Drinker's Dictionary, The
    (Franklin), 22–23
drinking habits, 17–19, 61–62,
    117–118
Drunkard's Progress, The, 61
drunkenness, 23, 25–26
Dukes of Hazzard, The, 158,
    161–163, 164
Duling, Paul and Hubbard, 87

Earle, Steve, 160
18th Amendment, 64, 71–72
Elliot, Bill, 176
Ellison, Brian, 136
*Enquiry into the Effects of
    Spirituous Liquors Upon
    the Human Body* (Rush),
    25–26
Enolmatic, 152
Esquire magazine, 102, 104
ethyl alcohol, 149
Evan Williams, 135–136
Excise Act (1791), 27

Faulkner, William, 122
fermentation, 144, 147
Ferrum Mercantile Company,
    79, 82
Figgins, Berle "Rusty," 134
flip (drink), 22
Four Pounds Flour (Lohman),
    17–18
Four Roses, 45
France, Bill, 97, 105
Franklin, Benjamin, 22–23

"Franklin County Moonshine"
    (Shepard), 161
Franklin County, Virginia, 72,
    73, 75–87, 119, 174
Free, Simmie, 7, 9, 15
French and Indian War, 23
Fulmer, Paul, 146 *ph*
fusel oil, 67

Gator, 163
Genna crime family, 71
Georgia Racing Hall of Fame,
    174
"Good Ol' Boys" (Jennings),
    162
"Good Old Mountain Dew"
    (Lunsford), 6
Grandpa Jones, 6
Grant, Ulysses S., 53
Greased Lightning, 98
Great Depression, 79, 85, 175
Grier, Pam, 98
Grogan, James, 175–176
Grosser, Jamey, 129–131

Hall, Roy, 7, 90 *ph*, 94, 95, 96,
    97, 105, 176
Hamilton, Alexander, 26–27, 38
Harding, Warren G., 66
Harlan County, Kentucky, 123
Haskell, David, 123, 124
Haynes, Roy A., 70
Heaven Hill Distilleries, 9, 45,
    135–136
Hickory Motor Speedway, 102
Hill, Henry, 21
Hillbilly: The Real Story, 129
Hillcoat, John, 80
Hillsboro, Ohio, 62–63
Hinton, Ed, 101, 104
Hodges, Pete, 77
Holt, Jack, 60
Honest Abe's Moonshine, 136
hooch, 14
Hoochinoo Indians, 14
Hoover, Herbert, 69, 71, 73
How to Mix Drinks (Thomas),
    22

hydrometer, 151

income tax, 44–45
*Inquiry into the Effect of
    Spirituous Liquors on the
    Human Body, An* (Rush),
    24 *ph*
Internal Revenue Service, 107,
    109 *ph*
International Review of
    Spirits competition, 10
Irishtown (Vinegar Hill),
    49–51, 53

Jack Daniel's, 131
Jackson, Alan, 160
Jacob's Ghost, 131
Jeff Brown & Still Lonesome,
    169
Jefferson, Thomas, 41
Jennings, Waylon, 162
Jim Beam, 45, 131
John Barleycorn funeral,
    64–65
Johnson, Annie Mae, 98
Johnson, Fred, 98
Johnson, L.P., 98, 100, 101
Johnson, Robert Glenn
    "Junior," 88, 97–98, 100–102,
    103 *ph*, 104–105, 125 *ph*,
    126–128
Johnson, Ruth, 98
Jones, Bug, 171
Jones, George, 160, 161
*Journal of the American
    Medical Association*, 67

Kaiser, Nathan, 134
Kazee, Buell, 142
Kentucky Bourbon Trail, 45
Kentucky Distillers
    Association, 45
Kentucky in 1800s, 43–44
"Kentucky Moonshine" (Pure
    Prairie League), 160
Kephart, Horace, 59
Kieft, William, 20
Kings County Distillery, 50,

124, 136–137, 138 *ph*, 139
ph, 140
Kit Brandon (Anderson), 87

LaBeouf, Shia, 80
Lakewood Speedway, 89,
94–96, 97
Landers, Starla, 169, 176
Last American Hero, The, 102
Law, Glen "Legs," 95
Lawless, 80
laws, alcohol, 19–20, 21–22,
23
lead poisoning, 66, 112, 117
Lee, Charles Carter, 72, 77, 78,
79–81, 86, 87
Lee, Henry, 38–39
Leonard, Elmore, 163
Lewis, Joseph J., 47
Liberty magazine, 84 *ph*, 86
Licensed Beverage Industries
Inc. (LBI), 107, 110
Lincoln, Abraham, 44–45
*Liquor Problem in All Ages,
The* (Dorchester), 21
Lohman, Sarah, 17–18
Lunsford, Bascom Lamar, 6
lye, 112
lyne arm, 147

Maclay, William, 27
MacQuarrie, Murdock, 162
Maker's Mark, 45, 131
Maker's White, 131
making cuts, 145, 149
marijuana, 118
Marshall, Jack, 154
mash, 144
Mayflower, 19
Mays, Clarence, 82
McCormick, Maureen, 163
McGee, Harold, 11–12
Me and My Likker (Sutton),
129
"Menace of 'Moonshine' Whisky,
The," 67
methyl alcohol, 145, 149
Michalek, Joe, 126–127

Midnight Moon, 125 *ph*, 126
Miller, Roger, 161
"Mississippi Mud" (H. Williams
III), 160
Mitchell, John, 39–40
Mitchum, James, 161, 163, 165
Mitchum, Robert, 154, 165,
166
mixology, 133. *See also*
cocktails; recipes
Molasses Act (1733), 21
Montour's Island, 41
Moon-a-rita, 10, 11
Moonrunners, 162, 163, 164 *ph*
moonshine, as term, 8–9
*Moonshine: A Life in Pursuit
of White Liquor* (Wilkinson),
120
Moonshine Blood, 162
Moonshine Conspiracy Trial,
79–84, 175
Moonshine County Express,
163
Moonshine Express tour, 175
Moonshine Festival, 175
Moonshine Kate, 161
"Moonshine Kate" (Moonshine
Kate), 161
"'Moonshine Man' of Kentucky,
The," 46 *ph*
moonshine poisoning, 66–67,
111–117
"Moonshine Still" (Holt), 60
Moonshine War, The, 163
"Moonshiner," 106
Moonshiners, 155–158, 167
Moore, Roddy, 80
Moose Shine Whiskey, 135
More Mountain Spirits
(Dabney), 15
Morgenthau, Henry, Jr., 85
Mount Vernon, 39 *ph*, 40–41
mountain dew, 14
Mountain Moonshine Festival,
8, 174
Muldoon, Dennis, 51

"Nancy the Moonshiner," 57–59

Nation, Carrie, 63
National Association of Stock
Car Auto Racing (NASCAR),
97–98, 102
Hall of Fame, 105
National Commission on
Law Observance and
Enforcement (Wickersham
Commission), 72, 75
National Motorsports Press
Association, 105
National Prohibition Act
(Volstead Act), 64, 71–72, 73
Neville, John, 29, 32–34,
36, 41
New Straitsville, Ohio, 175
New York Distilling Company,
50
Norris, Charles, 67
North Carolina Sports Hall of
Fame, 105
North Wilkesboro Speedway,
101

Ohio Whiskey War, 62 *ph*
Old Moonshiners of Georgia
Reunion, 169–171, 176
Oldman, Gary, 80
Ole Smoky Tennessee
Moonshine, 128–129
On Food and Cooking
(McGee), 11
Operation Dry-Up, 117
Operation Lightning Strike, 83
Osborne Brothers, 42
Ostrom, Matt, 157
Our First Century (Devens),
31 *ph*
Our Southern Highlanders
(Kephart), 59
Owens, Bill, 132–133, 134

Paintin' the Town Brown
(Ween), 6
Parkinson's Ferry, 35–36, 38
Parks, Raymond, 90 *ph*, 94, 97,
105, 176
Parton, Dolly, 128, 160

Paul, John, 79
Peach Blossom, 145
Phillips, James Atlee, 165
Phish, 42
Piedmont Distillers, 126–127
Pittsylvania County, Virginia, 155–156
Poison Moonshine Publicity Program, 112
Popcorn Sutton's Tennessee White Whiskey, 129, 131
Port Chilkoot Distillery, 8
Port Richmond, 48
Potter, Tom, 50
Powell, Chester, 169–170
Presley, Elvis, 165
Preventive Raw Materials Program, 108, 110
Prohibition, 61, 62, 64–73, 79
PROOF, 132 *ph*, 133–135
proofing, 151
Pryor, Richard, 98
Puck, 76 *ph*
Purdam, D. W., 55
Pure Prairie League, 160

racing, 89–105
raids, 48–51, 53
Rakes, Charles, 81
"Rapid Roy (The Stock Car Boy)" (Croce), 96
Raum, Green B., 53–54, 55–56
Reagan, Ronald, 104
recipes
    Bangin' in the Woods, 10, 11
    Flip, 22
    Moon-a-rita, 10, 11
    Peach Blossom, 145
    Spiked Lee, 133
    Red Devil lye, 112
    Red Hook, 50
Red Margaret, Moonshiner, 162
Redmond, Lewis, 153
Redmond's Hand Mash, 153
Redstone Old Fort, 36, 37
reflux stills, 150
"Revenooer Man" (Jackson), 160

revenue agents, 53–57, 68 *ph*, 69, 98, 100, 118–119. *See also* U.S. Treasury Department
Revolutionary War, 23–24, 26
Reynolds, Burt, 163
Richards, Jeff, 75, 77, 78, 81, 85, 87
Rittenhouse Rye, 135–136
Robinson, Edward G., 112
"Rocky Top" (Bryant and Bryant), 42
Roosevelt, Franklin D., 73
rum, 21–22, 23
Rush, Benjamin, 16, 24 *ph*, 25–26
Rushing, Jerry, 163

sales tax, 45
Sands Street, 49–50, 137
Saudi Arabia, 111
Saxon, John, 163
Schneider, John, 161
Scientific Temperance Instruction, 63
Scott, A. O., 80
Scott, Wendell, 98
Seay, Garnett, 91, 93
Seay, Lloyd, 7, 89, 90 *ph*, 91, 92 *ph*, 93–94, 97, 105, 176
See 7 Stars, 132, 134
7 Star Cooler, 131–132
Shade, Heather, 8
Sharpe, Willie Carter, 83, 85, 86–87, 175
Shepard, Jean, 161
slavery, 21
Smith, Jim, 75
Smith, Tim, 155, 156–157, 167
smuggling, 66, 69, 82–83, 85
speakeasies, 65–66
Speedway Park, 98
Spiked Lee, 133
Spoelman, Colin, 123–124, 136–137, 138 *ph*, 140
steam stills, 150
Steichen, Jeff, 134

stills
    seizure of, 68 *ph*, 69, 71, 107, 118–119
    types of, 150
Suchke, "Bullet" Bob, 173, 174
sugar, 81, 82, 91, 93–94, 95, 108, 110, 118
Sugar Act (1760), 22
Sunday, William "Billy," 64–65
Sutton, Marvin "Popcorn," 129, 130–131, 173
Sutton, Pam, 131

Tatum, Ben Kade "Junior," 118
Tavern Law, 131–132
taxes, 27, 29–32, 110, 151
"Tear My Stillhouse Down" (Welch), 160
temperance movement, 61–64. *See also* Prohibition
Tetens, Chris, 155, 156–157, 167
The Last One (*This Is the Last Dam Run of Likker I'll Ever Make*), 129
Thin Lizzy, 168
This Is the Last Dam Run of Likker I'll Ever Make (*The Last One*), 129
Thomas, Jerry, 22
Thompson, Eliza Jane Trimble, 62–63
Thorpe, George, 20
Thunder Road, 154, 163, 165–167
Tickle (person), 155
Tickle (TV series), 167
Tim Smith's Climax Moonshine, 157
Timberlake, Stephen D., 79–80
Town Branch, 45
transportation, 48 *ph*
triangular trade, 21
Trybox series, 135–136
Turner, Melinda, 57
turnip stills, 150
21st Amendment, 73

2bar moonshine, 132 *ph*, 133
2bar Spirits, 134

uisge beatha, 12
Unaged Tennessee Rye, 131
Uncle Tupelo, 106
*United States of America
    vs. Edgar A. Beckett et al.*,
    79–84
U.S. Treasury Department,
    99, 107
Alcohol and Tobacco Tax
    Division, 165
Alcohol Tax Unit (ATU), 75,
    108
See also revenue agents
usquebaugh, 12

Van Brunt Stillhouse, 50
Villanova, Arnaud de, 12
Virginia Department of
    Alcoholic Beverage Control,
    156
Vogt, Louis Jerome "Red,"
    94, 97
Volstead, Andrew, 64
Volstead Act (National
    Prohibition Act), 64, 71–72,
    73

War of 1812, 43
Washington, George, 23, 32, 35,
    36, 37–38, 39 *ph*, 40–41
Washington, Pennsylvania,
    175
Washington Distillers Guild,
    133–134
Wazeniak, Mary "Moonshine
    Mary," 67
Weavers, 142
Ween, 6
Welch, Gillian, 160
*Wettest County in the World,
    The* (Bondurant), 80
Wheeler, Wayne B., 64
whiskey, history of, 12–14
"Whiskey in the Jar," 168

Whiskey Rebellion, 29–41,
    31 *ph*
Whiskey Rebellion Festival,
    175
Whiskey Ring, 53–54
whiskey tax, 27, 29–32
white dog, 9
White Dog Whiskey, 134
white lightning, 9
White Lightning, 163
"White Lightning" (Jones), 161
White Whisky, 136
Wickersham, George W., 72
Wickersham Commission
    (National Commission
    on Law Observance and
    Enforcement), 72, 75
Widmark, Richard, 163
Wilcox, John, 143–145, 147,
    149, 151–152
Wild Turkey, 45
Wilkinson, Alec, 120
Willard, Frances, 63
Williams, Hank, Jr., 131
Williams, Hank, III, 160
Winthrop, John, 19
Wolfe, Tom, 102, 104
Women's Christian
    Temperance Union (WCTU),
    63
Women's Crusade, 63
Wood, Cheryl "Happy," 7, 9–10,
    14–15, 169, 173–174, 176
wood alcohol, 66, 67
Woodford Reserve, 45
Wopat, Tom, 161
worm, 147, 148 *ph*